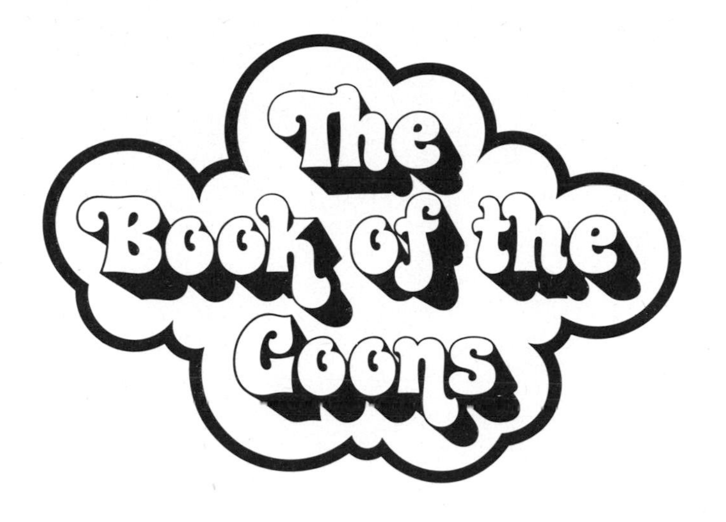
The Book of the Goons

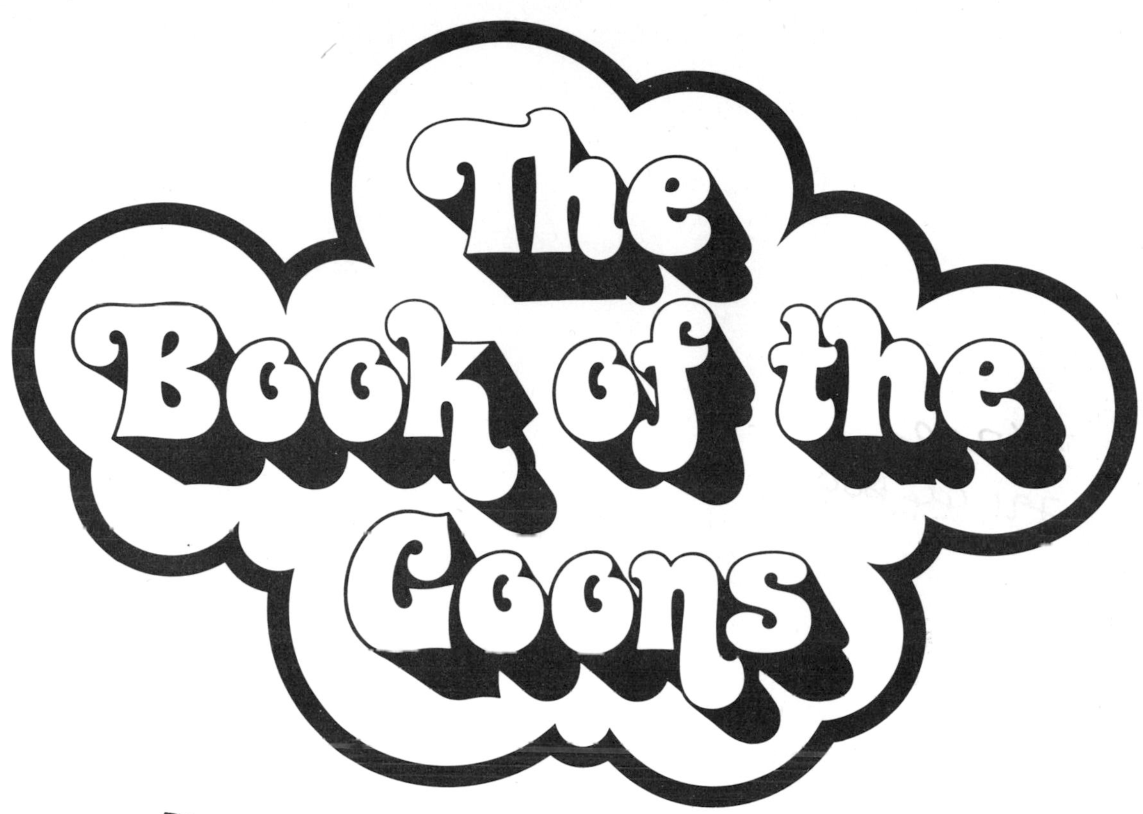

incorporating a new selection
of SPIKE MILLIGAN'S GOON SHOW SCRIPTS and,
by courtesy of Whacklow, Futtle & Crun
(Commissioners for Oaths, Threats Issued), the authentic,
unexpurgated inter-Goonal Correspondence
of Certain Naughty Gentlemen and Sundry Others,
alias Peter Sellers, Harry Secombe
and Spike Milligan, including photographs by Snowdon
and drawings by the Goons.

Robson Books

First published in Great Britain in 1974 by
ROBSON BOOKS LTD., 28 Poland Street, London W1V 3DB

ISBN 0 903895 26 9

The publishers acknowledge with thanks the
co-operation of the BBC.
Acknowledgements for use of photographs are due to David
Sim (pp. 40, 82, 84, 123, 135, 140, 141); to Thames Television
(pp. 6, 8, 87, 98, 100, 108); to *She* (pp. 125-7); to the *Acton
Gazette* (p. 93); to the BBC (pp. 11, 28, 59, 86); to The Press
Association (p. 19); to Keystone Press Agency Ltd. (pp. 15, 30, 47).

Editor Elizabeth Rose
Designed by Timothy Jaques FSIA

Printed in Great Britain by
REDWOOD BURN LIMITED
Trowbridge & Esher

Contents

Publisher's Note

The Goon Show letters included in this volume are part of the genuine correspondence that has been going on, in character, between the Goons over the past twenty or so years. They have not been edited in any way, save that on occasion real addresses have been removed to protect the innocent. The scripts, too, have been reproduced faithfully, complete with instructions for sound effects (*FX*) and for tapes (*Grams*).

We are most grateful to Lord Snowdon for allowing us to include some of the photographs he took at the special Goon Show recorded at the Camden Theatre, London, on Sunday, 30th April 1972 as part of the BBC's 50th Anniversary celebrations—also to Norma Farnes and Peter Eton for their invaluable help in assembling material, and of course to the Goons themselves for allowing us such ready access to their own collections of letters, drawings and photos.

Peter Sellers, Harry Secombe and Spike Milligan during the Thames Television version of 'Tales of Men's Shirts', August 1968

Foreword

When I was asked to write the foreword for this book I misunderstood what was required of me. 'Four words' I thought the publishers said, and with the speed of wit which helped to kill variety I wrote 'Please buy this book'. Presumably that was not enough, and here I am having to follow the last foreword author, a certain Royal personage. It's like following Beethoven's Fifth played by the L.S.O. with 'Three Blind Mice' picked out with one finger on a bad piano.

I don't see enough of the other two these days. The last time I spoke to Spike on the phone he was under the impression that I had been dead for two years. He even demanded a refund of £2 which he claimed he had sent towards a wreath. I came across Peter recently in the bowels of Broadcasting House. We embraced as Stanley and Livingstone must have done—an impression heightened by the presence of a coloured lady with a tea trolley. Then we dried our eyes and went our separate ways.

That's the way it is these days. We don't see each other for ages but when we do it's instant hysteria. It's a chemistry that never fails to work. The formula is to be found in this book. Take a piece of Eccles, a dash of Bloodnok, sprinkle with Ned, stir in a spoonful of Bluebottle, and stand well back.

Ned of Wales

alias Harry Secombe

Introduction

by PETER ETON

Some years ago, when the Goon Show was at its height, I had lunch with Spike Milligan. In the course of it Noel Coward stopped at our table on his way out, and I introduced him to Spike. 'Not Milligan the Goon Show writer?' said Noel. 'I can't begin to tell you how much I enjoy your programme.' Couldn't begin, maybe, but he tried. And I give you my word, he had tears in his eyes.

Later that day when I got back home, a five-year-old member of the household sat hand in hand with me and having asked for and obtained complete silence, listened with grim determination to *The Goon Show*.

Now, somewhere between the simple sophisticate and the blase child were (and are) the millions of admiring, fascinated, sometimes mystified, often bewildered but nevertheless loyal Goon Show fans.

I produced *The Goon Show* over a period of five and a half years—with time out to recover—from 1952 to 1956, following in the distinguished footsteps of Pat Dixon and Dennis Main Wilson. I had known the boys, including Michael Bentine, from their *Crazy People* days. As a features and drama producer, I had listened to them and admired their outrageous and totally original humour. Transferring to the light entertainment field, I asked if I might produce them, and they agreed.

In those days, there were three musical interludes —the Stargazers, jazz-harmonica player, Max Geldray, and the Ray Ellington Quartet, which left Spike only about fifteen minutes of script. This was all right for sketches, but wasn't long enough for a storyline to be developed. First the Stargazers departed, then Bentine left to pursue his own interests; and Spike, who had until then only written the show, began to take small parts. These gradually built up as he invented new 'voices'—such as 'Miss Throat', which on its first unscheduled appearance sounded exactly like a long and very rude belch. I was furious. Rounding on Spike, I bawled him out in no uncertain terms for interrupting the rehearsal, and deeply offended him. He had created this marvellous new voice, and all I could do was blow my top!

The show's audience began to increase with the introduction of a storyline. Hundreds of enthusiastic letters started pouring in from listeners, and our budget was increased. We began to achieve notoriety in the Press when Goon Shows asserted that the Albert Memorial had taken off for the moon, and that flying saucers have been seen over East Acton. (After that particular programme, hundreds of people phoned the BBC in all seriousness to say that they'd seen them too!)

Spike was expert at pricking the balloon of pomposity, and the storyline was usually a melodramatic and overblown version of a great drama or contemporary documentary. There was a period of topical subjects, such as 'The Sinking of Westminster Pier', which followed a newspaper report that Westminster Pier was indeed sinking inch by inch below the Thames. 'The Evils of Bushey Green' poked fun at the dispute then raging between the celebrated actor A. E. Matthews and his local council over the erection of a lamp post outside his home. Spike wrote this script in twenty-four hours and declared that it was 'an attempt to defend the right of the individual against the State'. He took the mickey out of my own book on Rommel's treasure with a Goon Show on the subject, and would often take popular novels and give them 'the Goon treatment'.

Unlike any other comedy programme of its time, *The Goon Show* was less a criticism of any social system than a bold and melodramatic rearrangement of all life. It was obliged to create a nightmare landscape of its own and to people it with men, beasts and machines terribly at variance with the observable universe. Some Goon Shows were merely disconcerting—if, of course, it is no more than disconcerting for an old woman to take an age of time to descend an apparently endless staircase to answer the door—in a bungalow! But most programmes were frankly devoted to man's crazily triumphant return to the trees from which he dropped.

The characters of the Goons' world were, until recently, in the minority—only very few golf club secretaries were as villainous as Major Dennis Bloodnok, M.C.; there must have been only one or two pimply boy scouts as obsessed by the love of play acting and consequent self-annihilation as Bluebottle; few people had two heads—but it is only too clear from the enormous success of the very last series of Goon Shows that these had become the dominant strain; that somehow, natural selection had reversed itself and our civilization would presently belong, once again, to the misshapen, the moon-struck, and the damned. As Dorothy Parker once wrote in a foreword to a collection of Thurber's pictures, it is interesting though not necessarily reassuring to speculate about the lives of the characters in a cartoon before and after that situation in which the artist has frozen them for our startled entertainment.

The thoughtful Goon Show addict will certainly wonder about the domestic life of those shambling, crumbling dotards Henry Crun and Minnie Bannister. What dark and shameful compulsion brought them together, the quaver-voiced, ruined one-time toast of the Indian Army and the doddering old oyster-sexer who, even now, is fitting out his umpteenth expedition to search for the International Christmas Pudding? What unspeakable rites united them, if wed they are at all? We know their coloured retainer Ellington at one time drove a phantom hearse; that their casually employed butler and part-time dustman, Headstone, was drummed out of the Tunderpawnee Chokadhas for taking part in an illegal floodlit Tattoo at the White City; and that Frothpump, another casual employee, in between bouts of lurgi, helped Mr Crun on his bath night. It is little enough; and we know still less about Comte Moriarty, the fugitive from Victorian gaslight, except that he is almost certainly a homicidal maniac.

However, as Mrs Parker was obliged to conclude about the Thurber men and their even odder women, it is madness in the end to try to provide great works of the imagination with sane and detailed backgrounds. One thing at least is certain: when the BBC invited people to send in their ideas of what the Goon characters looked like, an astonishing ninety-five percent of the listeners' drawings were alike—and corresponded to the Goons' own images of them. These characters had become as real to the listeners as they were to the boys, who even wrote to each other in character, as you'll see from the correspondence included in this book. Spike would often show me the wildly funny letters that he and the late Larry Stephens, who (like Eric Sykes) co-wrote some of the scripts, used to exchange.

The difficulties inherent in working with such talent and over such long periods made my life an exciting trial, though the Bumbling Bureaucrats of the BBC presented me with far more problems than the Goons themselves. Altogether I logged thirty attempts by them to stop the show. For instance, one week Major Bloodnok was awarded the OBE for emptying dustbins during the heat of battle—just after two BBC executives had received the honour. I was called up and warned about committing further breaches of taste. On another occasion, Peter imitated the Queen's voice during the hilarious launching of an attempt to dislodge the pigeons from Trafalgar Square, and I was hauled up again. The officials threatened to take the show off altogether in the face of this further example of 'rank bad taste'. I believe that it was only John Snagge's continued defence of the programme and insistance on Spike's right to freedom as a writer, which saved us.

Of course, there are many stories to be told about those shows, but one in particular comes to mind about 'The Terrible Revenge of Fred Fumanchu'. The script contains a simple, straightforward little sequence between Henry and Minnie and Ned, who keep locking themselves out of a house. The Goons played this scene very visually, and soon had the audience falling about helplessly. In fact, we recorded the longest laughter ever on a Goon Show—over four minutes—and as I edited it out later, Ben Lyon, who was editing a tape on a neighbouring bench, asked what I was doing. 'Throwing away laughter,' I replied. 'Don't do that,' he said. 'We're short of laughter this week. Give it to me.' And he edited it into *Life with the Lyons*.

I think we could do with some of that laughter today. The Goon Show should come back—the times are once again right for it. I saw a newspaper report the other day (and cut it out and sent it to Spike), about a German, Herr Willy Rolloff, who was arrested in Freiburg im Breisgau for 'firing his wife's dumplings at low-flying aircraft'. What more convincing evidence could possibly be needed? It is time that the Goons returned—time for a return to sanity.

The original team: Harry Secombe, Michael Bentine, Spike Milligan, Peter Sellers

TELEPHONES
01-123-4567

TELEGRAMS
CRUTTLE, LONDON

FUTTLE, CRUN & NEPHEW

SOLICITORS,
COMMISIONERS FOR OATHS

LINCOLNS INN FIELDS,
LONDON

THEODORE FUTTLE LL.B
HENRY CRUN
A. NEPHEW

SECRETARY,
MINERVA BANNISTER

YOUR REF: C/O/O/N/S

10th May 1974

Robson Books Ltd.,
28 Poland Street,
London W1V 3DB

Dear Sir or Madam,

We are instructed to warn you to erase from the relevant pages of your BOOK OF COONS the private and personal correspondence between Mr. P. Sellers, the well-known thing,and Mr. S. Milligan, the world-famous article, and return same to Major Denis Bloodnok (Rtd.), c/o YMCA, Tottenham Court Road, owner and trustee of important articles.

If you do not do this, another client of ours, a wrestler and policeman and Kung Fu expert, will be forced to close with you.

Respectfully,

LCrun.

Larry Crun

Correspondence

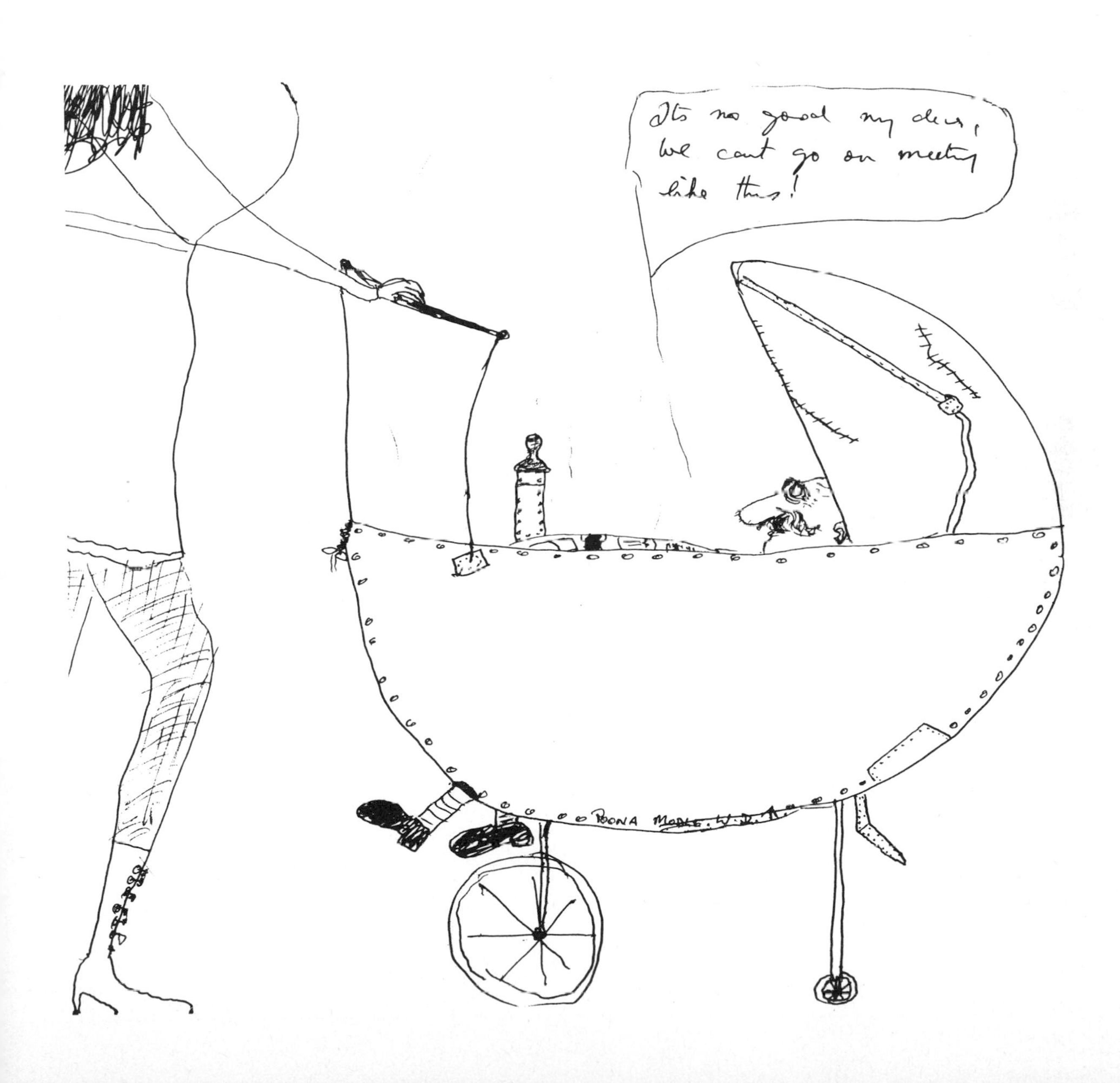

MESSRS CHEW, THREATS AND LID
(Chemists and Abortionists by Appointment)
3 Squirm Street
Grey Friars.

Sir,

We have been informed of your apparent striction in the Colonic channels.

Let us as remedial apothecaries forward you our new and powerful "abort". Fruits De Badiane, a secret remedy extracted from an impotent Nargar coolie in 1812.

We hope the contents will prove beneficial to you and we can always supply you with a heavy duty quality.

Yours respectfully,
For and on behalf of:

Mrs. Ethel Rotts

WIGGLE AND FRUIT
(Solicitors for Oaths)

Dear Sir,

Whereas let it be known that the area known as Harry Secombe is to be sold in lots by public auction at the Sutcliffe Arms at Beaulieu.

If the sale of the area known as Harry Secombe does not fetch the reserved price of £800. (Eight Hundred Pounds) then the area known as Harry Secombe will be pulled down and turned into blocks of flats.

Whereas you are a shareholder in the area known as the Harry Secombe, we would be pleasured by any instructions you may have regarding the disposal of your area, id est; the hanging portion of the trouser seat, known as Shining place and/or The light in the East. If you wish your area of the Harry Secombe to be untouched and unsullied and remain in the brown belt, then will you instruct your solicitors accordingly.

Yours respectfully,

Mr. Nules.
For Wiggle & Fruit.

P.S. The proceeds of the sales will go to the Estate of the late Lady Clarissa Bloodnok by order of Major Dennis Bloodnok. M.C.C.

P.P.S. The motivation of the pulling down of the Harry Secombe was instructed by City Council Survey who condemned the Harry Secombe as unfit for human inhabitation or socks.

TELEPHONES:
NUGENT 4728.

TELEGRAMS:
BLEIOUH. LONDON.

WHACKLOW, FUTTLE,
& CRUN.

SOLICITORS.
COMMISSIONERS FOR OATHS.

LINCOLNS INN FIELDS,
LONDON.

HON. SEC.
MILLICENT HIGGS.

OSCAR WHACKLOW.
THEODORE FUTTLE. L.L.B.
HENRY CRUN.

June 4 1952.

YOUR REF. GALAH/ILL/OOH.

Dear Sir,

re:- 13A Hornton Close

We have heard from your Landlords Solicitors, Messrs. Frutbone, Fruitnagel and Welk that you are desirous of vacating the above premises. As you are aware, your Agreement was for a period of not less than 6 (Six) Calendar Months at a rental of £9-9-0 (Nine Guineas) sterling per week.

Your having guaranteed all such monies to be paid in advance.

Under the TOWN AND COUNTRY PLANNING ACT, 1743 (Sub-section 4, paragraph 8) it is laid down that rentals paid in advance can only be refunded to the occupant in the case of him, her, them or they sub-letting the premises to another person or persons.

Miss Catchpenny informs us, however, that she is quite prepared to release you from your agreement subject to your calling upon us at our offices and signing various deeds, documents, etc., in our presence.

Further, we would point out that the Speaking Tube, was installed in the above premises at great expense for the use of words and not liquid refuse.

Yours faithfully,
For and on behalf of
WHACKLOW, FUTTLE AND CRUN

Henry Crun.

HENRY CRUN.

TELEPHONES:
NUGENT 4728.

TELEGRAMS:
BLEIOUH, LONDON.

WHACKLOW, FUTTLE, & CRUN.

SOLICITORS.
COMMISSIONERS FOR OATHS.

LINCOLNS INN FIELDS,
LONDON.

HON. SEC.
MILLICENT HIGGS.

OSCAR WHACKLOW.
THEODORE FUTTLE, L.L.B.
HENRY CRUN.

June 10 1952.

ESTABLISHED LONG BEFORE 1632!

YOUR REF. MMM/NMP/NUCK.

Messrs. Clunes, Froth & McBread,
Brannockburnstrausse,
Edinburgh
WILTS.

Dear Sirs,

We are in receipt of your Mcscroll of the 9th. (ninth) instant.

Regarding Madame Bannisters' Ducking Stool; we understand from our client that he has paid all he intends to pay on this particular chattel. We have, in our possession, a document signed by Madame Bannister, saying that she was in urgent need of a new commode and was quite prepared to exchange her Ducking Stool for the above mentioned article. As Commodes of the size required are extremely difficult to obtain we suggest that the matter is dropped forthwith and that there be no further correspondence on this subject.

With regard to the burning of Mr. Peter Sellers. We have had considerable correspondence with him regarding this and he suggests that Mr. Sconce Firge takes his place next Thursday and no one will be the wiser. Colonel McBloodnok, we hear, is at present suffering from acute fong and will hand the distribution of tickets over to the Earl of Felt.

Colonel McBloodnok's Fruit Leopard is to be on view at the Vicar of Dung's Garden Fete together with some Nut Lions and a Coptic Mule, the proceeds will go to Major J.D. Grafton's Barnard Recovery Fund.

Mr. H. Crun expresses a strong desire to attend the broadcast performance of one of the Coon Shows and would be most pleased if Mr. Jimmy Costa could obtain some tickets for him. He is a keen listener to the 'Ray's It From Brading Show.'

Yours faithfully
For & on behalf of
WHACKLOW, FUTTLE & CRUN.

Henry Crun
HENRY CRUN

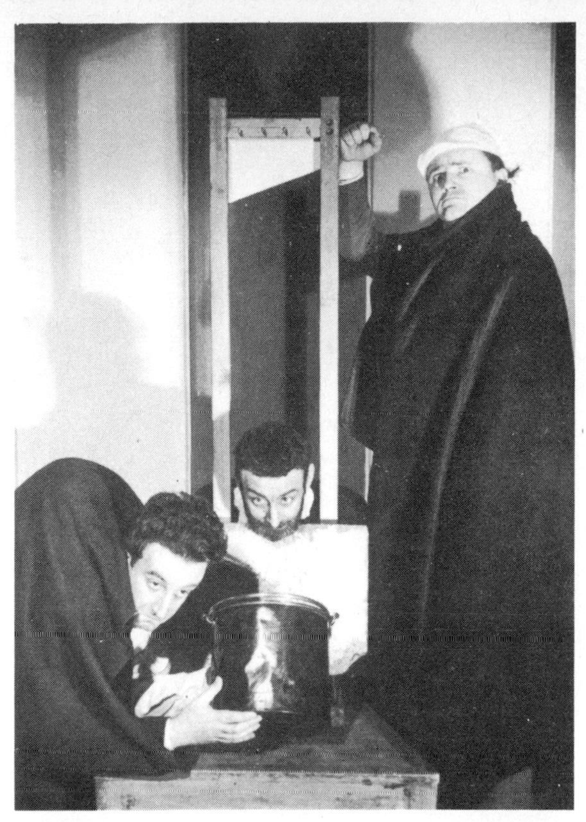

Ray Ellington, Peter Sellers, Spike Milligan, Harry Secombe

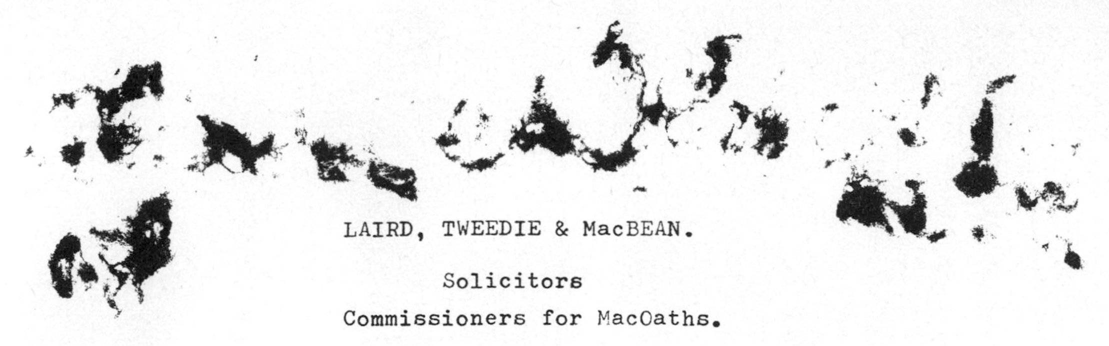

LAIRD, TWEEDIE & MacBEAN.

Solicitors

Commissioners for MacOaths.

4, Angus Clyde,
Shortcake Street,
BRAEMAR.

August 25, 1952.

Dear Mr. Milligan,

We have been approached by our Client, Mr. Peter Richard Henry Sellers, who is at present residing at the Caledonia Hotel in the City of Aberdeen, to forward to you a copy of the works of the great Poet and Tragedian, William MacGonnagall.

We hope, dear sir, that you will find many hours of infinite delight as you peruse the pages of the enclosed volumes. Remember, dear sir, :

"A better poet was never seen in the City of Dundee at any time,
And never again shall be as far as I can see in the meantime;
His poem on the Tay Bridge is most beautiful to be read,
As I found by reading it one cold night before I went to bed.
Among the poets of the present day, there's none on earth who
can possible be able for to gainsay,
But that William MacGonnagall, poet and tragedian,
Is truly the greatest poet that was ever found above or below
the meridian."

Mr. Sellers has been wont for to imitate the works of the great master, (not for him to gainsay!) and has therefore ordained that this short "gem" should be included in our letter:

'Terence Milligan is a writer and actor and poet of high degree,
Which is surely plain for all to see,
Gainsay it I dare anyone who can,
Because T. S. Milligan is a good zany man.'
(William McGonagall, alias Peter Sellers) →

Terence Milligan!
is a writer and actor
and poet of high degree
Which is
for all to see
it I'd dare anyone
who can, because
a good man
William McGonagall

-2-

"'Twas on the 25th. of August in the year 1952,
That the Rev. Henry Crun felt that his acquaintance with
the City of Aberdeen was due for renew;
So without delay, at Kings Cross station, he embarked and the
train left on time,
Because had he walk d to Aberdeen, it would have taken him
months nine!
When the Rev. Crun arrived there he found it was most
beautiful to behold,
Also the theatres, alas for which the seats were all sold,
And after having walked around the streets in the freezing cold,
He decided that perhaps it was not so beautiful to behold.
Messrs. Clunes, Froth and MacBread whose offices were in the
Union Street,
On seeing the Rev Crun received a grand treat,
And they were resolved from him to extract what money they
could,
So as he passed by their window they gave him a resounding
smack on the head with a huge lump of wood.
This caused him to cry out in pain and much agony
And hurriedly offer up prayers to Saint Hagony!
He then retreated with great haste to a mountain glen,
And the spectators noticing that there was nought else to see,
****ed off home again!

We would like to know if you would be interested in some genuine Highland Heather , Rare old mountain goat droppings and Welkin Rings. We hasten to assure you that should you see fit to place an esteemed order with us for any of the aforementioned articles they will be despatched to you without delay or dismay.

We are, dear Sir,
Your humble and obedient servants -
LAIRD, TWEEDIE & MacBEAN.
Harris Tweedie
HARRIS TWEEDIE.

12th February 1957

Dear Harry,

Thank you very much for your book.

Unfortunately, we are at present out of stock of the appliance you requested, but it will be forwarded to you in the plain wrapper in due course.

Yours sincerely,

THIRK VOLUNTARY.

Secombe to Milligan

Counter No.

POST OFFICE
INLAND TELEGRAM
FOR POSTAGE STAMPS

Serial No.

Chargeable words	Sent at/By
	8/57
Charge £	Circulation

\+ 7 8.40 VIGILANT CN 59

To SPIKE MILLIGAN UXBRIDGE ROAD W12 =

I INTENDED INDULGING IN A SPOT OF CLAIRVOYANT READING THIS WEEK BUT NOW YOU HAVE SPOILED IT STOP THERE IS NO JUSTICE AS A PRISONER REMARKED WHEN THE COURT CONVENED WITHOUT THE JUDGE THIS TELEGRAM IS COSTING ME A FORTUNE BUT YOU KNOW ME MONIED JIM LOVE AND KISSES HUGH JAMPTON + +

Counter No. .... POST OFFICE INLAND TELEGRAM FOR POSTAGE STAMPS Serial No. ....

EALING B.O. 26 FEB 57 W5

Chargeable words	Sent at/By 6/P
Charge £	Circulation
Actual words	

165 5.45 VIGILANT CN 22

To SPIKE MILLIGAN UXBRIDGE ROAD W 12=

HAVE YOU FINISHED THIS PAGE I WANT TO TURN OVER

LOVE= EDGAR WALLACE

+130 W 12+

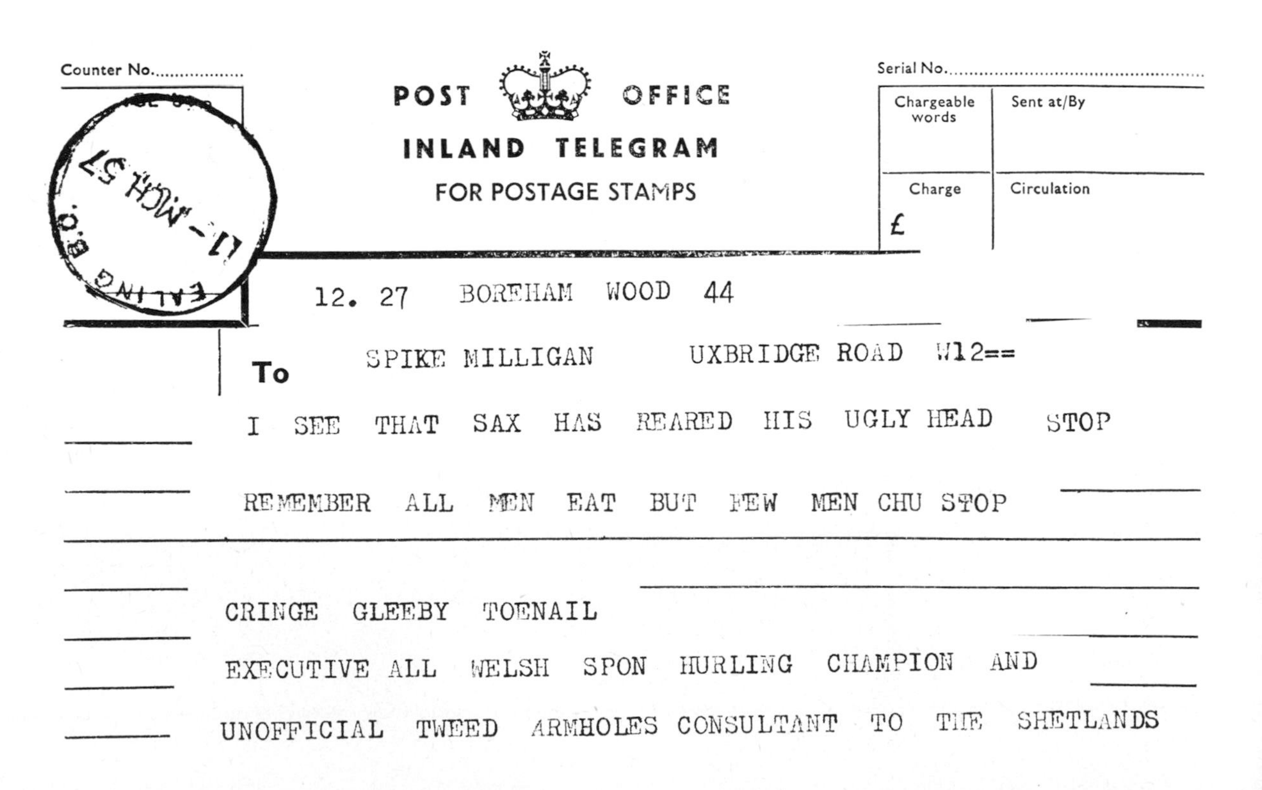

Counter No. .... POST OFFICE INLAND TELEGRAM FOR POSTAGE STAMPS Serial No. ....

EALING B.O. 11 MCH 57

Chargeable words	Sent at/By
Charge £	Circulation

12. 27 BOREHAM WOOD 44

To SPIKE MILLIGAN UXBRIDGE ROAD W12==

I SEE THAT SAX HAS REARED HIS UGLY HEAD STOP

REMEMBER ALL MEN EAT BUT FEW MEN CHU STOP

CRINGE GLEEBY TOENAIL

EXECUTIVE ALL WELSH SPON HURLING CHAMPION AND

UNOFFICIAL TWEED ARMHOLES CONSULTANT TO THE SHETLANDS

Michael Bentine, Spike Milligan, Peter Sellers, Harry Secombe

5th March 1957.

Dear Cringe Glebly,

Of course I remember you. I am enclosing a picture of the Junior Lunatics' Rock-Eating Outing at Ketelby Marshes. If you scrutinise our dear headmaster under a magnifying glass, you will see that little fault in vision which caused his untimely death under a steam-roller.

Yours respectfully,

P.S. Please return photograph - to me if possible.

Secombe to Milligan

YOUNG ST. B.O.
19 MCH 57
KENSINGTON W.8

Coun......

POST OFFICE
INLAND TELEGRAM
FOR POSTAGE STAMPS

Serial No.

Chargeable words	Sent at/By
	7 55
Charge £	Circulation

XW 3231 26 9. 34 VIGILANT CN

To SERGEANT MILLIGAN 2 KENSINGTON W8=

= FIRE +

2 W8 + + XW 3231

Secombe to Milligan

Counter No.................

YOUNG ST. B.O.
19 MCH 57
KENSINGTON. W.8

POST OFFICE
INLAND TELEGRAM
FOR POSTAGE STAMPS

Serial No.....................

Chargeable words	Sent at/By
Charge £	Circulation

908 3.45 PM GULLIVER XN 21

To SGT MILLIGAN KENSINGTON AW8 =

MOVE ONE DEGREE REPEAT AND WATCH MY MESS TIN

NEXT TIME = ANGRY JIM +

2 W8

Milligan to Secombe

Counter No.................

Office Stamp

POST OFFICE
INLAND TELEGRAM
FOR POSTAGE STAMPS

Serial No.....................

Chargeable words	Sent at/By
Charge £	Circulation

Prefix	Handed in	Service Instructions	Actual words

If you wish to pay for a reply insert **RP** here

BLOCK LETTERS THROUGHOUT PLEASE

To HARRY SECOMBE

HAVE CAPTURED RHINE CROSSING SINGLE HANDED STOP

STRANGE LACK OF ENEMY RESISTANCE STOP

HAVE DUG IN ON NORTH BANK OF NIEMEGEN

SGT MILLIGAN

Sent 19 March 1957

The particulars on the back of this form should be completed.

Secombe to Milligan

Counter No.................

YOUNG ST. B.O.
19 MCH 57
KENSINGTON. W.8

POST OFFICE
INLAND TELEGRAM
FOR POSTAGE STAMPS

Serial No.....................

Chargeable words	Sent at/By
Charge £	Circulation

906 3.45 PM GULLIVER XV 17

To SGT MILLIGAN KENSINGTON W8=

NEIMEGEN LLOYD GEORGE COMPLETELY DESTROYED

WELL DONE = PLEASED PERCE +

2 W8 NEIMEGAN

15th September, 1960

Dear Sir,

Find enclosed a new allround "Min" tubular steel commode support, invaluable on yachts, moored rowing boats, unlevel floors and for irregular bowel habits – thousands of testimonials from satisfied customers.

"During the 1932 earthquake in Quetta, I found this a great comfort and managed to remain seated throughout the seismographic upheaval."

Signed.

Major Bloodnok.

Can also be had in brown oak – send for full details.

Signed.

Herman Ludge.

23rd September, 1960.

Dear Peter,

At last! The enclosed cutting from the Racing Motor of 1927 has unwittingly printed a photograph of the actual moment that Grytpype-Thynne first set eyes of Count Moriarty. The caption that goes with the picture was "An attempt by Grytpype-Thynne to cover the names of the people concerned".

This photograph is history, do not lose it.

(Signed) Jim Nine. (9)
for and on behalf of:
Tom Twelve (12).

Producer Dennis Main Wilson, Jimmy Grafton (at whose pub the Goons used to meet), Milligan, Larry Stephens; in the background: Secombe, Bentine, Sellers

9th December, 1960.

Dear Hairy,

Thank you for the steaming lunch, wine and chit-chat.

See you during the next hunger period.

Yours

JIM TYPHUS .

10th December, 1960.

Dear Ned

Stench of burning socks, a pox, a plague and a panic on you, these Quons and Quins that you forced me to partake in the heat of a Chinese Dining Room, went ill with me and I was stricken with the bilateral kwott, it rolled from the ankles at dawn and by mid-day was speeding up the shins towards those noble piles the knees.

As I speak great diaramas of flaming vests are raining from the sky, incinerating the trilby caps of vagrant carters. For this relief much thanks, and to hell with Burgandy.

15 April 1964

To the Mug of Arloo:

You'll never get me Arloo, you swine, because I too have got you heavily insured!! So we shall see who's the first to collect.

Bim - bam - bala - boo - Bloodnock!

Bumble Bee Bong.

17 April 1964

Dear Eccles and Neddy:

I want to thank you for all them wishes. What it is that you sent to me on the Kelloggs boxes. I've cut the wishes out and am wearing them with stickey plaster to reinforce the bends.

I don't like this game but I shall be back to East Finchley soon.

I say to you, love and electric twits and things.

Plonge

Blune Button

BEVERLY HILLS,
CALIFORNIA

OR % HANKS SNAKE HOL
POONTANG SHACKS
PICATAN.
INDIAN
COUNTRY

DEAR Uncle Grytpype –
When I gotted
yore letts I was so pleased to hear
that you & the famous Count Moran
-nobility was coming to seee me. I
am sending you my check what I
have got tew make the defraying
easy for you. Also I have got
you both the VEEP sweet at
the Worldif astria like you sed.
The pills that Mayer Bloodnok sent
me made me go all funny in
my littlue bed & I was put in
in the hospittle. They said I had
eten poisen but I no that

2

dear Mayer Bloodsuch would
not want to killed me.
anyway I'm orlight now &
I'm staying at Hanks Snake
House & he is kind to me.
I wont to come home to E. Finchley
I dont like it heere. I do
hope you & the famos Count are
working along Her Majesty. It must
be fun, with all them garls.
Well I will close now
& hope you ~~&~~ the famos
count will rite agan.

love

Blullottle

Beverly Hills, California

Sellers to Milligan

May 22, 1964

My dear ~~Mr.~~ Count Moriarty:

I trust you will not be unsettled by this note, so to speak from the blue, and that it will not disturb your daily routines, but I was given your name by an old acquaintance of mine that I met out here in the Americas. A colonel Grunt of the 14th U.S. Cavalry. He has informed me that certain areas that are in the vicinity he has under his control, so to speak, have large amounts of usable oil buried in them, just waiting to be drawn.

However, he does need a go-ahead person like yourself, together with my own talents, which in all modesty I can claim are numerous, and I was wondering whether you felt you had spent enough time in the company of Mr. Hercules Grytpype-Thynn. I happen to know you have been associated with this particular gentleman for numerous years and that things at the moment may not be succulent for you, as I sometimes am wont to describe things.

No doubt you have heard of me. I served in Her Majesty's Royal Deserters during the Sepoy rising in India, and apart from mild attacks of dysentery which come upon me from time to time, I am in fine shape.

Should you be interested, dear Count, please contact me at your earliest possible convenience. And remember me to your knees, which I trust are keeping well and apart.

I am your humble and obedient servant,

Dennis

Dennis Bloodnok, Major, Ret.

23rd June 1964

H.G. Pype, Esq.,
and Count J. de Moriarty,
c/o Spike Milligan, Esq.

My dear Estemmed Sirs,

I am in receipt of your hand written letter which I have just had read to me, by my aged sister, Flora GRILLNIK, who never married you know and still retains the FAMILY name. So of course do I-Emil GRILLNIK.

Our father was a french leather worker who came to Dover one night on the spree and took away with him in his naughty little boat a fair English miss, who later gave birth, I am sorry to say, in the boat. As you will see and realise, esteemed Sirs, we have no connection in any way whatsoever with the name of Bloodnok. Having served HER MAJESTY in various capacities all over the Globe, I am distressed by the continual threatening letters I receive from various people who claim that I am this SCANDALOUS SCOUNDREL AND BAWDY MAN Dennis Bloodnok.

So, Gentlemen, you will obviously realise there has been a serious misunderstanding and I can assure you and am prepared to swear, being a religious man on my old photographs, that I am not anything to do with Major Dennis Bloodnok, and although I do bear a striking resemblance to that ignoble person, it's only a resemblance in feature not in heart.

Many times when out walking, I have been nearly run to ground by various HOOLIGANS who mistook me for this cheap skate because of my physical likeness and I tell you, dear Sirs, it's becoming very tire some especially for an old man like ME.

Perhaps I could prevail upon your good selves to suggest some method of protection to prevent my DEAR SISTER and I from being attacked any further or being mixed up in any way with this villainous He-DEVIL Bloodnok. Of course, under the circumstances you will realise that as I am no relation whatsoever I cannot send you a cheque for £60. 0. 0. (forty nine pounds) because I am, as I said before nothing to do with anyone except me.

Sincerely,

Flora & Emile

EMIL GRILLNIK.

10th August 1964

Dear Mr. Milligan,

I am a poor old lady, living in retirement in a corner of England, and I have just received through the post, a photograph of a gentleman, bedecked with medals, and wearing a toupe and large moustache. Why you should want to send this form of photograph to me, a poor old lady living in a corner of England, I have no idea. I have been a poor old lady for some years now, and I trust I shall continue to be so, and to remain unmolested by people of your sort. I just wish to spend the rest of the time the Good Lord has left me, with my old photographs and the little money my poor dear husband bequeathed to me.

I am, unfortunately, completely bald due to loss of hair, and have now been able to secure the services of a crepe hair wig, kindly loaned to me by the Old People's Crepe Hair Wig Association and Minge Fund. This, however, has given rise to several rumours that I am a female impersonator, and bear some other name. Also, because I am of rather portly appearance due to old age, undesirable rumours have been circulating that I am pregnant. This is, of course, a tissue of lies, and I deny it all, do you hear me Sir, I deny it all. We are just good friends. Should you have any old funds at your disposal, that you no longer need, I should be very grateful of them, as I am suffering rather badly from certain things.

Please remember, Sir, that I am nothing to do with anyone that you may know, and am purely and simply a poor dear old lady in the evening of her life, living at the mercy of the elements in a corner of England. So kindly don't send me any more rude postcards, as I find them most disturbing. Also, I can read between the lines - an art I learned during my years in India. I was there as a dear old lady of course.

I am, Sir, yours modestly and faithfully,

Cecilia Blonule

Cecilia Blonule.

TYPED BY A FRIEND IN THE CIVIL SERVICE.

31st August 1964

Dear Mr. Grytpype Thynne & Count Constable 96,

In case you have never heard of me, my name is Rex Finchley, Private Investigator, specialising in divorce procedures, re-arrangements and other situations that need constant surveyance and certain things.

I have been handed your letter by a dear old lady, living in retirement in a corner of England. When I visited her, she was suffering from acute shaking of the knees, and advanced diarrhoea. She made a pathetic figure, sitting in a stained bed, counting what I call pubic hairs, immediately recognisable to my trained eye as being of French origin. I managed to glean from her feeble mutterings that she was heavily worried by the letter she had just received from you and the Count Constable 96, enclosing said hairs. Now then, good Sirs, I can assure you that I have perused every inch of her poor old frail cottage, and I can find not a single trace of anything military or any military person or shred of evidence to suggest that anyone ever connected with the Army or any of His Majesty's Services had ever placed foot in its frail old dear walls. Your suggestion that a certain military gentleman was living at her frail address with certain railway monies is absolutely ridiculous, do you hear me, ridiculous I say. Nothing more than untrained poppycock. This poor dear old lady would not allow any train monies anywhere near her, and shakes at the mere mention of the word military - it would make your kind hearts bleed to see her poor old frame quivering with fear when the name of ~~[illegible]~~ anybody at all is mentioned. She in fact has not used any of His Majesty's trains for many years because of her aforementioned diarrhoea and other complaints. She has to be within easy reach of a commode due to her condition. I am still continuing my investigations, and I can find no trace of anything military or old army photographs in any part of this poor old dilipidated cottage. I will at once inform you and the Count Constable 96 and your team of G.P.O. representatives and friendly official trained experts, so that you may come down yourselves and be witnesses to my thorough and trained searches. While ~~the said~~ my searches are in progress, this poor dear old frail lady will be withdrawing to her cousin, the Laird of Hairs' country seat in the Tulloch of Tools, so that I may have complete freedom to investigate every corner of her dear old dilapidated cottage. I would not advise you gentlemen to journey up to the Tulloch of Tools, as it lies in the remotest part of the Outer Hebrides, and one has to have a constitution of cast iron - nay - steel to survive in such a bleak spot. Also the Laird of Hairs is fiercely unsociable and has hated the French and English since birth. It speaks very well of my client that she intends to suffer such hardships purely to clear her name of these dastardly accusations, which continue to pour in from certain parts of the British Empire and other places.

I have collected the hairs which you so kindly sent to this poor dear old lady, but find they are five short of the 30. I am wondering whether, if I returned them to you unused, you would be so kind as to let her have a refund, which would amount, if my arithmetic is right, to approximately 8/4d. These monies are needed by this poor old lady to help her reach the Tulloch of Tools, which as you know, is in the Outer Hebrides, and should not be visited by anyone in any circumstances.

Should you, gentlemen, have any further investigations that you need carrying out, I should be very pleased to put you in touch with an excellent Private Detective by the name of

Sergeant Eccles. He is a fine intelligent man, and I can recommend him thoroughly to you. You will just need to be a little patient with him, but your patience, I may add, will be richly rewarded. He comes complete with a newspaper and wooden fruit box in which you need to put some earth or a few cinders, and he will be as happy as the day is long. Just so long as he knows where to go in an emergency. He is as clean as a whistle and twice as lively. He likes marbles.

Awaiting a favourable reply from you Gentlemen. I can be reached for the next week or so c/o Rope F, Rowton House Buildings, Camden Town, London, N.W.1.

Rex Finchley.
REX FINCHLEY.

TELEPNONES:
NUGENT 4728
TELEGRAMS:
BLEIOUH, LONDON.

WHACKLOW, FUTTLE, & CRUN

SOLICITORS,
COMMISSIONERS FOR OATHS

LINCOLNS INN FIELDS,
LONDON.

HON. SEC.
MINERVA BANNISTER

OSCAR WHACKLOW
THEODORE FUTTLE L.L.B.
HENRY CRUN

YOUR REF. COONS

24th February 1967

Dear Mr. Milligan,

Captain Arthur Bloodnock, brother of the notorious Major Dennis Bloodnock, but not, I am sorry to say, a participant in the latter's fame and fortunes, has managed to persuade his brother to temporarily loan to him the enclosed modern tape, on which you will find a rehearsal of white coons, re your letter of 20th February 1967.

Would you be so good as to have a carbon copy made of it, and return the original to our good selves. If you fail to comply with this request, things may go badly for you.

I am, Sir,

Your Obedient Servant,

Crun

Henry Crun.

A letter received by Sellers dated July 28, 1967 from an American lady offering a race horse for sale stimulated the following exchange of letters:

Sellers to Milligan

August 7, 1967

Dear Jim:

As horse dealers of repute, Moriarty and I have advised this dear lady not to sell, pending your inspection of her stable wares. Thank you for ancient neddograph bound in rare leather.

Milligan to Sellers

14th August, 1967

Dear Sir,

I have had your nice letter passed on re the American Horse.

I am a cat butcher and I collect meat for cats. I see that Mrs Bogley wants 15,000 gns for the horse, if she doesn't sell him I would be willing to put in a bid somewhere in the region of £8 which I think would afford me a reasonable profit on my pussy-cat meat.

I also sell minced cats to horses who are no longer vegetarians. This is a new idea which is catching on in Desert countries. If you have any old cats that have shot their bolt if you could pack them in brown paper parcels and send to Tom Daft, Horse Food Refinery, Newcastle-on-Tyne.

Sincerely,

Tom Daft.

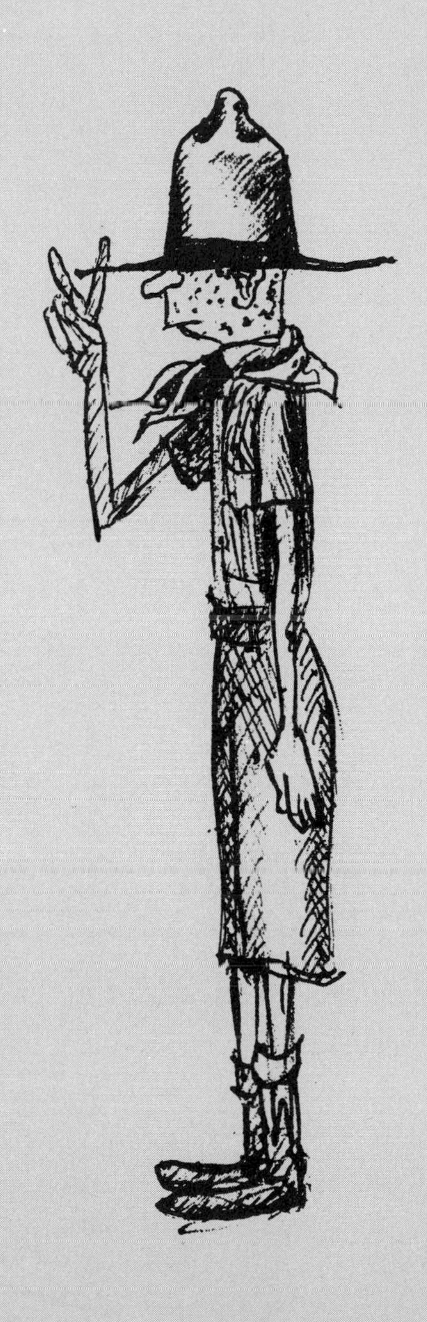

Sellers to Milligan

Via WESTERN UNION **CABLES**

RECEIVED 18 DEC 67

94 1/48

PC418

LD207 L LLK085 INTL FR TDL BEVERLY HILLS CALIF ~~98 1/50~~ 18 1259P

EST WS 195

SPIKE MILLIGAN MERMAID THEATER
LONDON (ENGLAND)

LOOK HERE YOU NAUGHTY MAN WHATS GOING ON OVER THERE. I WAS LOOKING THROUGH ME OLD PHOTOGRAPHS AND I SAW THAT YOU ARE DUE TO DEPICT THE CHARACTER OF BEN GUNN AT TREASURE ISLAND ON MERMAIDS. I ONCE HAD A RELATIVE WHO LIVED ON THE ISLAND BY THE NAME OF MERVYN BLOODNOK A POOVE BUT NOBODY IS PERFECT AS YOU WELL KNOW ANYWAY HE FELT NO PAIN. I HOPE YOU HAVE A GRAND OPENING TONIGHT AH THATS BETTER. YOUR OLD FRIEND AND COMMANDING OFFICER

DENNIS BLOODNOK OF THE AMERICAS
(11).

WESTERN UNION INTERNATIONAL INC.

Milligan to Sellers

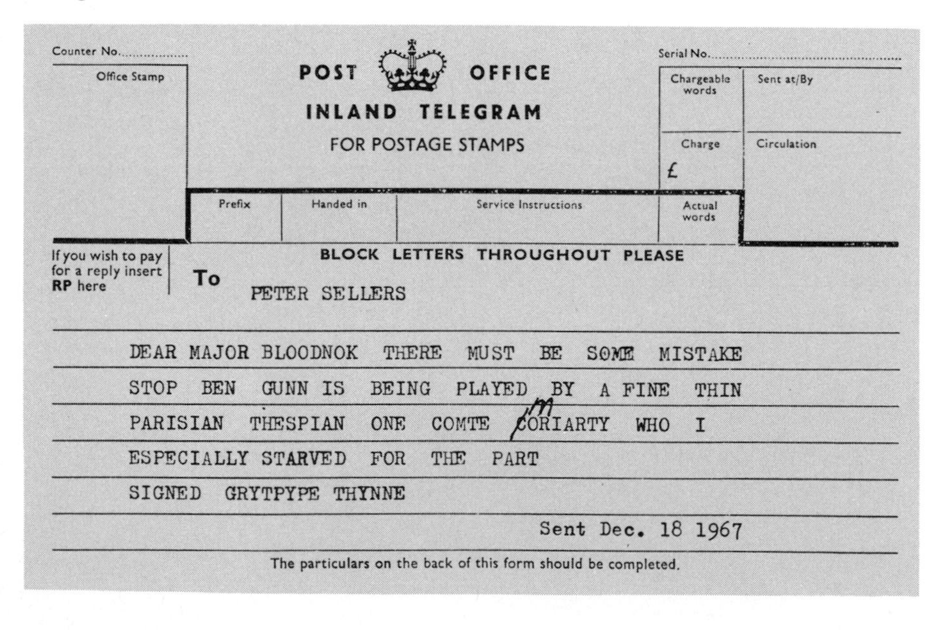

Counter No.................. Serial No.................

Office Stamp

POST OFFICE
INLAND TELEGRAM
FOR POSTAGE STAMPS

Chargeable words	Sent at/By
Charge £	Circulation

Prefix	Handed in	Service Instructions	Actual words

If you wish to pay for a reply insert **RP** here

BLOCK LETTERS THROUGHOUT PLEASE

To PETER SELLERS

DEAR MAJOR BLOODNOK THERE MUST BE SOME MISTAKE
STOP BEN GUNN IS BEING PLAYED BY A FINE THIN
PARISIAN THESPIAN ONE COMTE MORIARTY WHO I
ESPECIALLY STARVED FOR THE PART
SIGNED GRYTPYPE THYNNE

Sent Dec. 18 1967

The particulars on the back of this form should be completed.

Via WESTERN UNION CABLES

PB717 LA576

L LLY273 INTL TDL BEVERLY HILLS CALIF 55 8 945A PDT

LT SPIKE MILLIGAN BAYSWATER LONDONW2 (ENGLAND)

75

LOOK HERE SIR HOW DID YOU KNOW I WAS IN CALIFORNIA STOP
ACTUALLY I AM IN LOWER MONGBOOLA BUT IT LOOKS AMAZINGLY
LIKE CALIFORNIA STOP LOVE FROM A SIMPLE PERSON WHO BARES
A SMALL RESEMBLANCE TO DENNIS BLOODNOK BUT IS IN FACT
NO RELATION WHATSOEVER.

MONGBOOLA .
(41).

RECEIVED 19 DEC 67

WESTERN UNION INTERNATIONAL INC.

4th March, 1968

Peter Sellers Esq.,

San Moritz
SWITZERLAND.

WICKLOW. FUTTLE & CRUN.
SOLICITORS AND COMMISSIONER
FOR OATHS.

Dear Sir,

Regarding the back payment of rent from 1926, from your client Major Dennis Bloodnok.

You will remember you said he had died defending the G.P.O. tower from the Arab attack. We give you the lie, Sir. Major Bloodnok is now living in a Military Dairy in Poona, disguised as a Guernsey Heifer.

We would appreciate if you could contact him and ask him for the payment of monies he owes.

Respectfully,

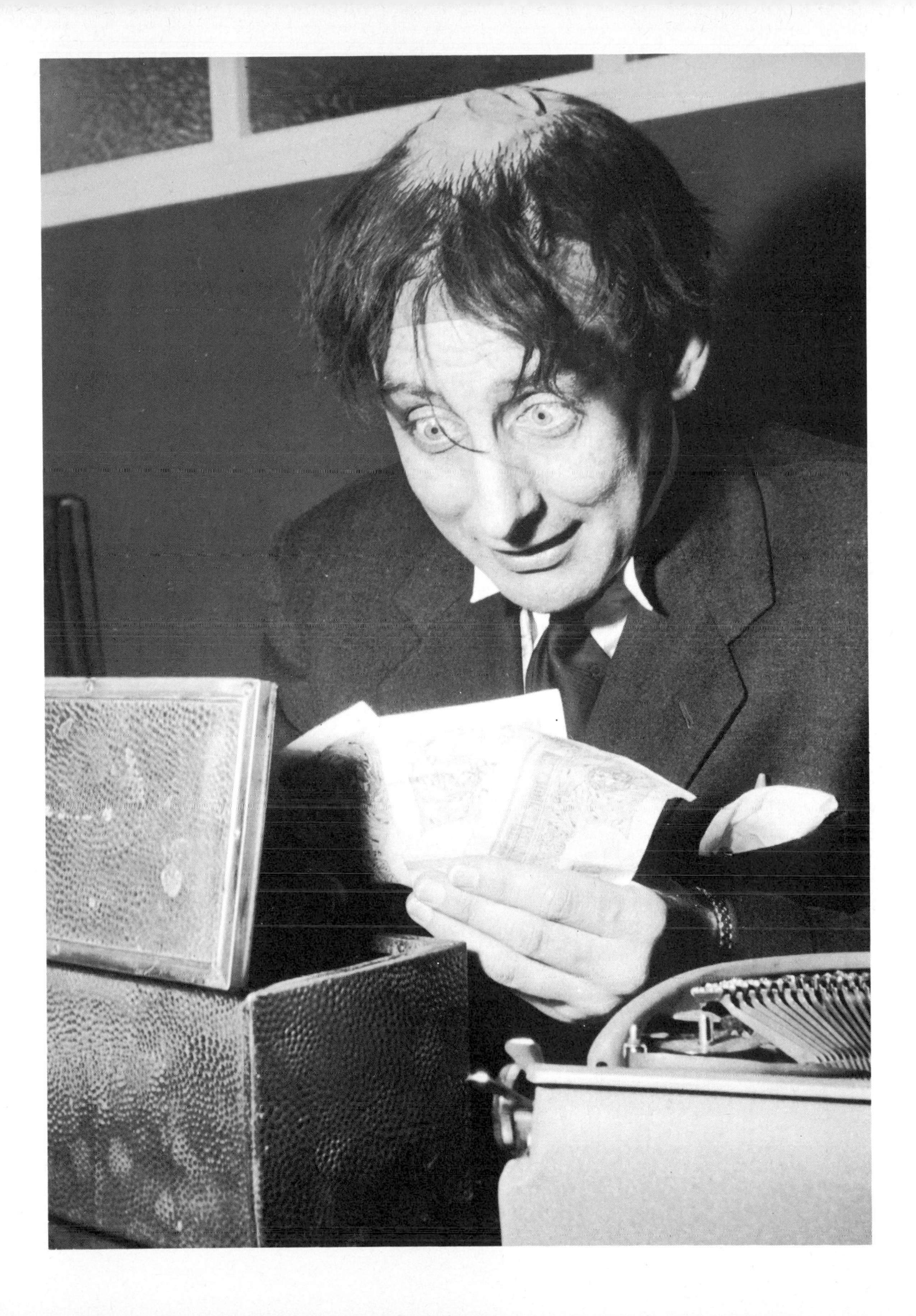

SNOPISTE, KRUTCHWARMER unt GESÄTCH,
Schweitzerlors Doktors für Oads
Temporary offidzen: St. Moritz.

7 März, 1968

WICKLOW, SUTTLE & CRUN,
Solicitors & Commissioners for Oaths,

Dear Fron Sirs,

Ve have zer estemt geplugen ledder from your offidzen vot iss in zer arrival of zer Schweizerposten, unt ve are replying unter Schweizerlors for our steamed klient Herr Peders Ellers zer vell known Britisch tax evader.

Pliss know dat zer terrible man of Brown Obermajor Denise Bloodnok iss still unter zer siege of Colonel Nassers fiendisch Egyptian forces unt other turbanned devils in zer GPO tower, also dat he iss in a mind to retreat to zer Albert Memorial unt konzolidate one of his positions behind zer Princes head unt shoulders where he can commant his boy scout forces with power unt Ralph Reader.

Unt now ve giff you back zer lie vot it voss given by you to us! Dat naudy man vot iss living in Poon in zer disguise of zer Maharishi yoghurt iss zer notorious French amateur untertaker Count Villion de Paprikon Moriarty! He iss living unter zer power of zer Englischer skoundrel of konfidenz unt curry G. Thin. Zese rodden men have kaused our klient Herr Peders Ellers unt Der Bloodnok much kopfschmertzen unt angst. He iss telling us dat he ohs no rent from 1926 or 1927 unt unter zer Schweitzer Milk Chokolate Lors he iss living free of zer rent in zer GPO tower until zer Arab attacks halt, or until for merely a nominal sum he can camp at zer back of Prince Albert for zer retreat of Browns. So zer lie goot sirs iss on zer other boot.

Yours with yodel unt respekt,

Kürt Krütchwärmer

Kurt Krutchwarmer,
for unt on behalf of
SNOPISTE, KRUTCHWARMER unt GESÄTCH

Zer 12^{tit} of der Marze.

Herrn. Speke Millington

Dere goot zeir—
let this rare
Sweitchesgewels welkomen you
tu der land of edelweis.

From your Sweinlaugen.

Fort Fwatchwarme

St. Morrys Snow Bar
and All Night Crevice.

27 March.

Dear Major Bloodnok,

The Compte di la Compte di Villion de Paprikon Moriarty, has requested I reply to your rude military letter which arrived in the Scheitcherposten Eilsendung this morning. Were it not gor the fact that he and his partner The Hon. Alpine Thynne, St. Morrys Teachest and Bogging Champion, are at present instructing The Char of Percy, Mrs. Mable Throng, Colonel Nasser and the famous Elizabeths Tailor on the use of their famous newspaper skis, he would I know give you a lash of his acid and-~~stinking~~ stinging gallic wit. Therefore be thankful sir that you have not received one of The Counts french letters, and should there be one more military insult He will sendung to YOU.

Yours trooly,

Miss Stanes.

Coral Browne - Stanes.
Secretary to Thynne Enterprises

Milligan to Sellers

21st March, 1968

Peter Sellers Esq.,
St. Moritz,
SWITZERLAND

Dear Sir,

How dare you send me dung by Express Post. If you are not careful Eil sen dung to you by surface mail.

Bloodnok

'Bloodnok McBloodnok in a leisure moment. To Spike from Pietro' →

MORIARTY AND THYNNE

Licensed Co-Respondents

2nd May, 1968.

Dear Mr. Milligan,

We are very sorry to have to trouble you with this trifling matter, but our client, Mr. Pewter Sailors, has sent you in error a cheque for £200 of Her Majesty's sterlings, which, if cashed at any known bank, would cost you and our client considerable embarrassment. Therefore, the Count Moriarty, "the well-known amateur C.B.E." and myself have taken this opportunity to forward to you under the same cover this genuine cheque for 200 pounds worth of sterlings, which can be cashed immediately we are in receipt of the afore-mentioned cheque, which was sent to you, as I have already pointed out, in error by our well-meaning but simple-minded client. Should you be in any doubt as to our credentials, Major Dennis Bloodnok has seen them on many occasions, and although he is at present in Poona under siege in the military dairy, he would, I am sure, find time, even in this distressing situation, to gladly testify as to our means.

Meanwhile, dear Sir, please let us have the cheque as quickly as possible, and just as soon as it is in our hands, wewill release certain monies and make them available to you on presentation at any good village post office of this remarkable piece of paper that you will find enclosed.

We are, dear Sir, your obedient servants,

The Rt. Honourable Hercules Grytpype-Thynne

Compte de la Compte di Geraldo de la is Moriarty
Weedkiller Extraordinary to Sam Spiegl and
King Hussein of Jordan

Round House,
Camden Town.

P.S. Enclosed please find photographs of our new yacht lying at anchor in Monte Carlo harbour. She's a fine sea-worthy craft capable of boy scout knots per hour. Should you wish to leave the country due to embarrassments with the Inland Revenue, this fine vessel can be anchored within the hour just off Pevensey Bay within easy reach of the sea.

(35th april 1968)

Burkley's Bank promise to pay the bearer of demand the some of Two Hundred Moriarty moneys.

£200#obo.

D. Bloodnok
Officer i/c Funds.

c/o A Corner of England

Dear Raucaus / Take this genuine gift from a poor silly old military man who in a weak moment - foolishly imitated your great strains of Melody. Take no further action I beg you AHHIOUEEOON (excuse me) & leave a poor old man of war who has served his country in peace. Take this £10 to any police station & they will let you have it. Love to you & the ball

Dennis Bloodnok V.C. V.C.

TELEPHONES:
01-123-4567

TELEGRAMS:
CRUTTLE, LONDON

FUTTLE, CRUN & NEPHEW

SOLICITORS,
COMMISIONERS FOR OATHS

LINCOLNS INN FIELDS,
LONDON

THEODORE FUTTLE L.L.B
HENRY CRUN
A. NEPHEW

SECRETARY.
MINERVA BANNISTER

YOUR REF.

27th May, 1968.

Dear Mr. Milligan,

Owing to the sad demise of your old and highly esteemed friend, Oscar Whacklow, Mr. Pewter Sailors has taken it upon himself to have this new paper printed, incorporating young Nephew. He hopes that you will accept this small supply as an indication of his unmitigated regard, to enable business to carry on as usual (or as usually as possible).

As I believe you are well aware, Mr. Sailors is now all at sea aboard his worthy craft, steaming at 400,000,000 knots per five-day-week in foreign tiddler-infested waters. He is, of course, still endeavouring to recover from the sudden, if hardly ill-timed, tragic departure of your afore-mentioned late lamented colleague.

I am, dear Sir, your (and his)
humble servant,

Yours,

Henry Crun.

Milligan to Secombe

13th January, 1969

Dear Ned,

So now it's a flat in town, eh! Naughty Neddy.

Jim Crapologies.

P.S. Sorry about your Hobson's.

Milligan to Secombe

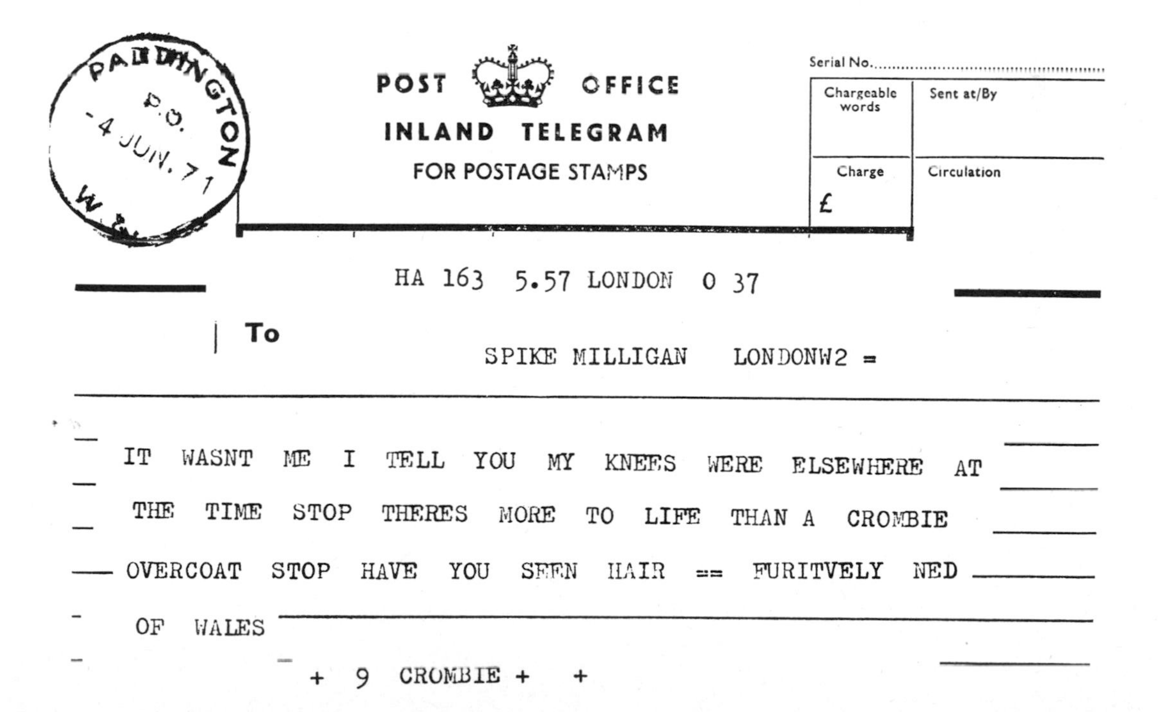

PADDINGTON P.O. -4 JUN. 71 W.2

POST OFFICE
INLAND TELEGRAM
FOR POSTAGE STAMPS

Serial No.
Chargeable words | Sent at/By
Charge £ | Circulation

HA 163 5.57 LONDON 0 37

To SPIKE MILLIGAN LONDONW2 =

IT WASNT ME I TELL YOU MY KNEES WERE ELSEWHERE AT THE TIME STOP THERES MORE TO LIFE THAN A CROMBIE OVERCOAT STOP HAVE YOU SEEN HAIR == FURITVELY NED OF WALES

+ 9 CROMBIE + +

17th August, 1972

My dear Neddie,

How dare you write such a brilliant piece to go into the Goon Show Script Book.

You realise, of course, that you are masking my true genius as a writer, by proving your genius as a writer. You will be hearing from my solicitor. You shall also be hearing from the young woman who appeared on the bill with you at the Birmingham Empire in 1921, who was known to have entered your dressing room in between acts, and subsequently agreed to charge for her dressess. The implication is obvious, you are in fact trying to hide behind this breakfast, and also I am afraid owing to your enormous bulk, your hiding place is known. Come out with your hands up, and your legs down, and in that order.

You will be hearing from my solicitor about this.

Congratulations.

Count Moriay.

P.S. You will be hearing from my solicitor about this.

Secombe to Milligan

PADDINGTON W.1 E.O. 23 MAR. 73

POST OFFICE
INLAND TELEGRAM
FOR POSTAGE STAMPS

Serial No.
Chargeable words | Sent at/By
Charge £ | Circulation

R 48 3. 18 LONDON T 27

To SPIKE MILLIGAN 9 W2 =

YOU DIDNT HAVE TO TAKE UP THE CUDGELS ON BEHALF
OF YOUR SOCKS THEY CAN STAND UP FOR THEMSELVES
= CARDINAL WOLSEY +

9 W2 + TSO TGMS LNAP +

'Moriarty the pickings are good over here and the Free Press makes a fine overcoat for a nippy day. Missing you – Gryt.' →

FREE PRESS
THREE YEARS OF THE FREE PRESS
Has The Freep Gone 'Establishment?'
The pickings are good over here
& the Free Press
makes a fine
overcoat for a
nippy day
missing you

PETER SELLERS
HARRY SECOMBE &
SPIKE MILLIGAN

The Camden Theatre, Sunday 30 April, 1972

BBC Radio 4 presents

THE GOON SHOW

Specially written for the 50th Anniversary of the British Broadcasting Corporation by SPIKE MILLIGAN
Produced by JOHN BROWELL

Dramatis Personae

Hercules Grytpype-Thynne	A plausible public school villain and cad	PETER SELLERS
Mate	Drains cleared while you wait	
Bluebottle	A cardboard cut-out liquorice and string hero	
Major Denis Bloodnok	A military idiot, coward and bar	
Henry Crun	A thin ancient, and inventor	
HARRY SECOMBE	*Ned of Wales* *Neddy Seagoon* *The Houses of Parliament*	True blue British idiot and hero always
Eccles	The original Goon	SPIKE MILLIGAN
Count Moriarty	A French scrag and lackey to Grytpype-Thynne	
Minnie Bannister	Spinster of the Parish and inseperable from Henry	
Ellinga	Batman to Bloodnok, singer and what-have-you	RAY ELLINGTON
The Conks	Dutch nose swinger and harmonica player extraordinaire	MAX GELDRAY

Orchestra conducted by PETER KNIGHT

Assistant to Producer Martin Fisher. *Production Secretary* Anne Ling. *Sound Team* Eric Young, Maggie Dean, Mardi Eyles, Michael Cowles.
Original members of the Wally Stott Orchestra – Trumpets Alan Franks, Freddy Clayton, Basil Jones, Stan Roderick, Tommy McQuater.
Trombones George Chisholm, Lad Busby, Jack Armstrong, Don Lusher. *Saxes* Bob Burns, Frank Reedy, Harry Smith, E. O. Pogson, Bill Povey, Ken Dryden. *Harp* Osian Ellis, David Snell. *Percussion* Jock Cummings.
The Ray Ellington Quartet Dick Katz, Judd Proctor, Ian White, Bill Eyden.

THE GOONS

Historians of the future will find it difficult to lay the responsibility for the Goons at any one doorstep. A Westminster hostelry, the *Grafton Arms*, could well at some time in the future carry a blue plaque to the effect that 'Goonery Was Brewed Here'.

Spike Milligan was the presiding scriptural genius – although during the long life of the Goons both Eric Sykes and Larry Stephens wrote a number of episodes. And Spike, with fellow Thespians Peter Sellers, Harry Secombe and in the very early shows, Michael Bentine, breezed life into the fantasies of Goonery.

Con Mahoney
Head of Light Entertainment, Radio

Part of the BBC's souvenir programme for their special 'reunion' Goon Show – the first for twelve years – at which Lord Snowdon took the photographs appearing on the following pages (65–75).

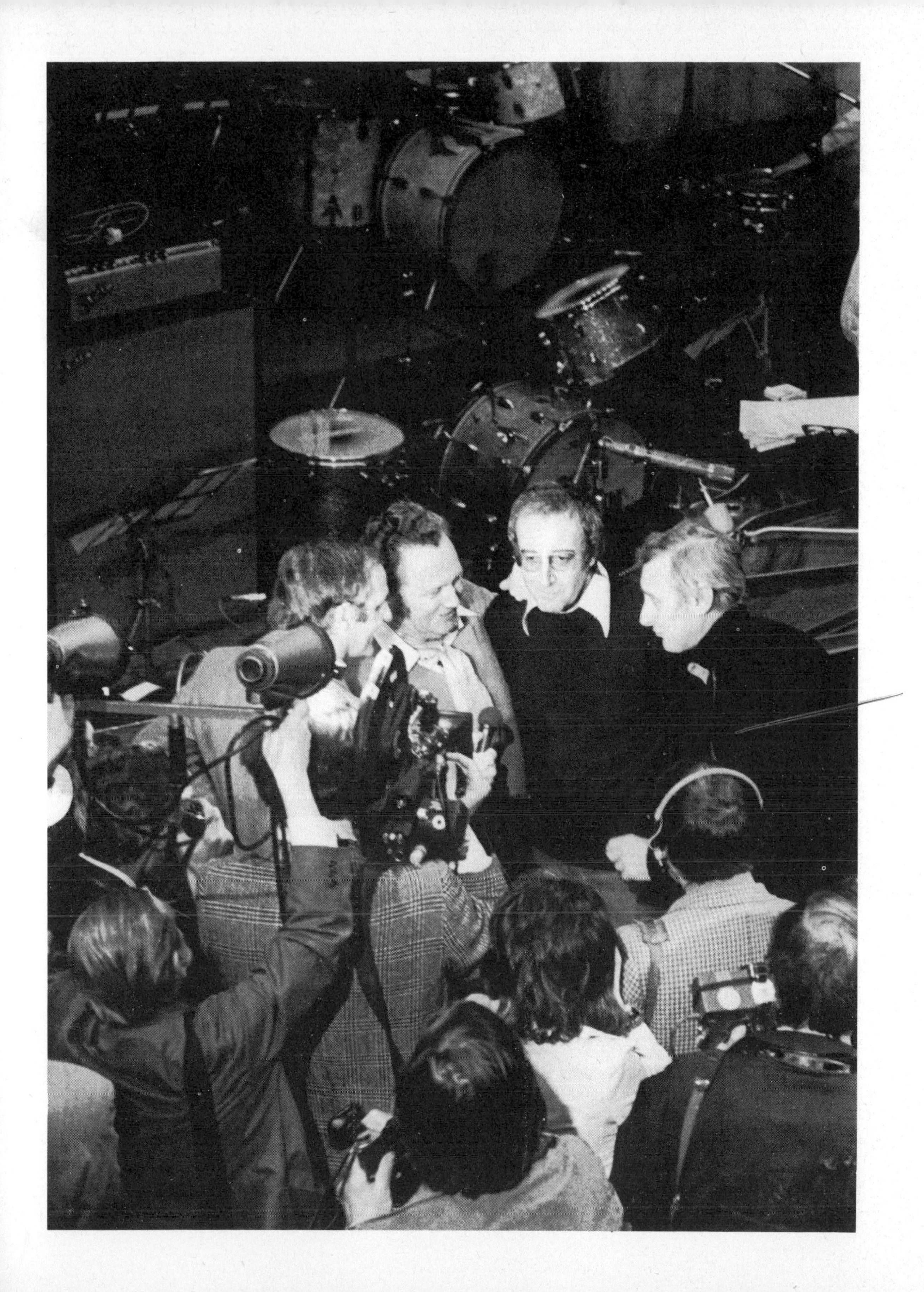

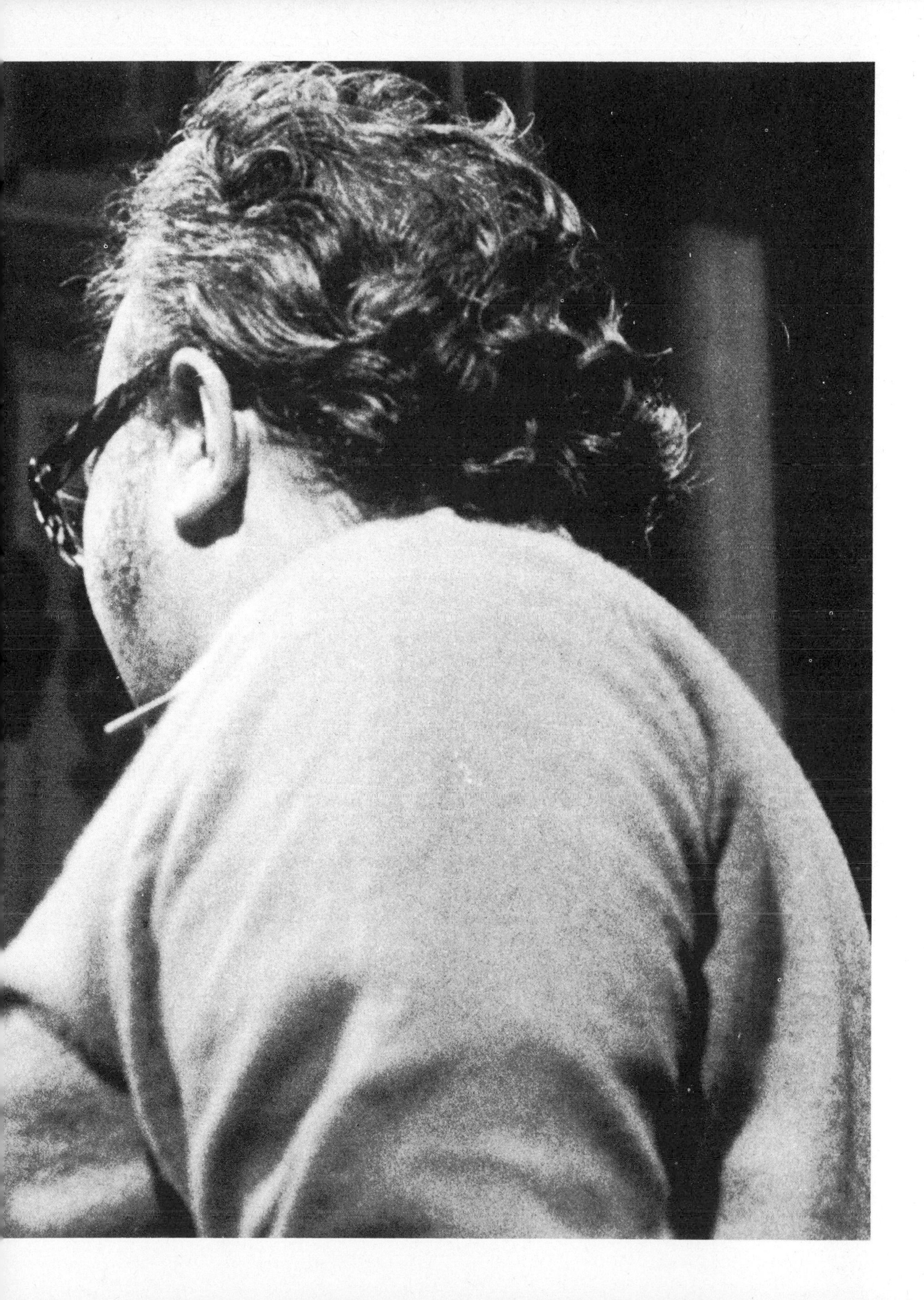

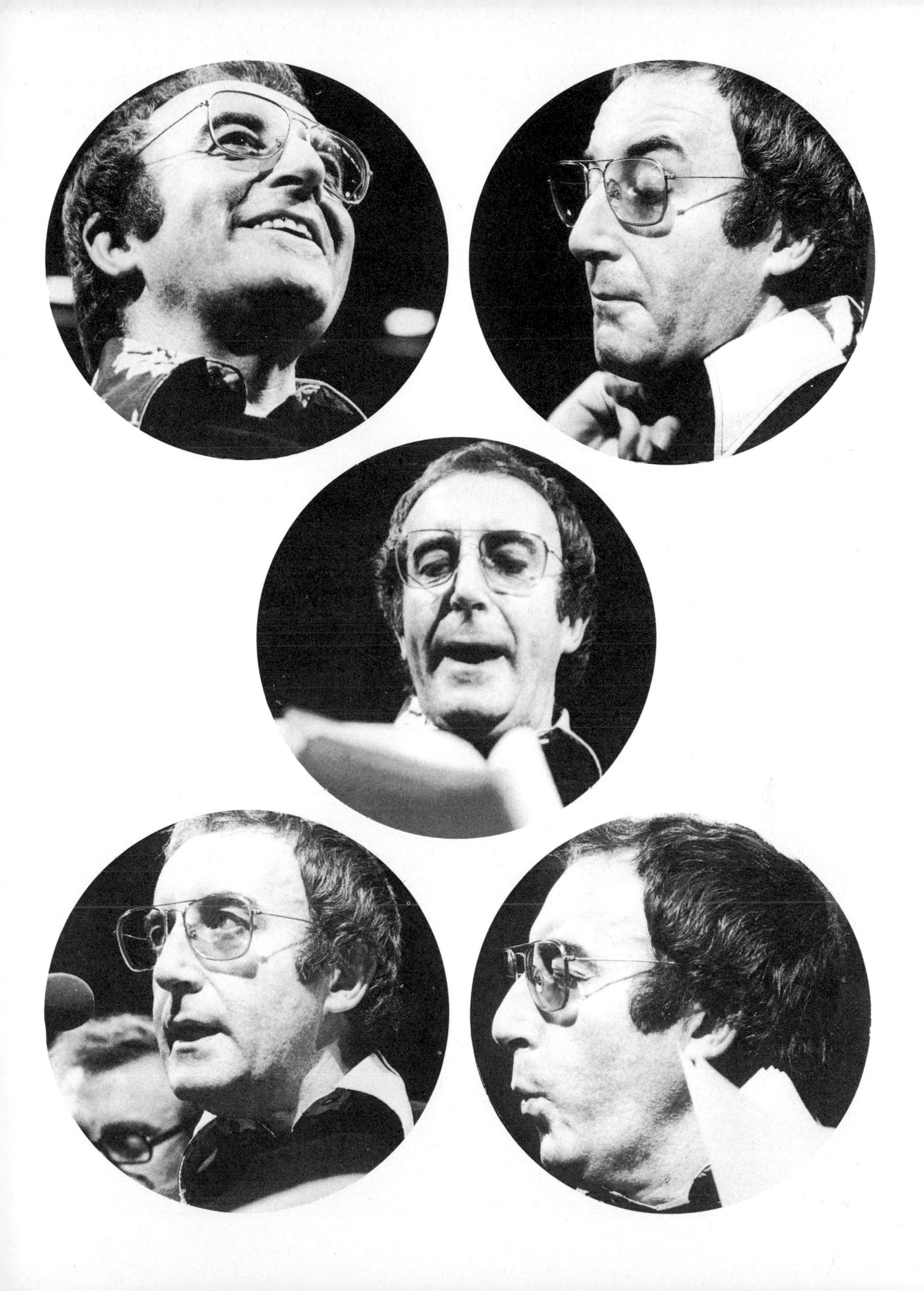

CHAMPAGNE
12 BOTTLES

MOET

A sort of Glossary

JIM SPRIGGS
a kind of strangulated voice that Spike used, pronounced 'Jeem'.

LITTLE JIM
a high-pitched child (played by Spike) who lives in Eccles's boot, and is thought to be his nephew. He points out when people have 'fallen in the water'.

TWITT (EARNIE SPLUTMUSCLE)
an idiot voice used by all three Goons.

SWEDE
a very rustic voice, based on a character whom Peter met in Sussex at the home of producer Peter Eton.

GERALDO
a kind of Cockney-Jewish voice used by Peter, based on the late bandleader's voice.

FLOWERDEW
a 'camp' voice used by Peter and Spike.

SINGHIZ LALKAKA (THINGZ)
BABU BANAJEE
two Hindus, played by Peter and Spike.

FRED BOGG
a Cockney idiot played by Harry.

BENTINE
a professorial voice based on Michael Bentine's Professor Osric Pureheart, who was a character in the original *Crazy People* show which developed into *The Goon Show*.

CYRIL
based on a friend of Peter and Spike.

HERN SALES or ERNEST HERN
a solemn, humourless American news announcer voice, used by Peter.

LEVIS
a voice used by Harry, based on Carroll Levis.

AFRICAN CHIEF
voice used by or based on Big Chief Ellinga (Ray Ellington).

HUGHIE GREEN
voice used by Harry, based on the TV personality and quiz-master.

IZZY
one of Harry's 'voices', based on the Jewish comedian Izzy Bonn.

DIMBLEBY
a commentator-type voice, used by Peter, based on Richard Dimbleby's.

ROCHESTER
a grating, negro voice based on Eddie Anderson, who played a coloured retainer of this name in *The Jack Benny Show*.

OLD DEAR
a quavering 'duchessy' voice, used by Peter.

'IT'S CHOCOLATE TIME'
a breathy female voice used by Peter, based on a contemporary advertisement for hot chocolate.

The Terrible Revenge of Fred Fumanchu

(Series 6)
Transmission: Tuesday, 6 December 1955
Studio: The Camden Theatre, London

CAST

Peter Sellers

Patsy Hagen
Major Dennis Bloodnok
Grytpype-Thynne
Henry Crun
Bluebottle

Spike Milligan

Fred Fumanchu
Throat
Moriarty
Minnie Bannister
Eccles

Harry Secombe

Chief Commissioner Neddie Seagoon

With The Ray Ellington Quartet, Max Geldray,
and the Orchestra conducted by Wally Stott.
Script by Spike Milligan.
Announcer Wallace Greenslade.
Producer Peter Eton.

WALLACE
This is the BBC Home Service. Now here is a record.

Grams: Scratch. Wallace (Pre-Recorded) Saying 'This is the BBC Home Service.'

WALLACE
We present the Eddie Calvert of the East, Fred Fumanchu and his Bamboo Saxophone.

PETER
But let us turn back the clock to the year 1895 – the year of the Great Exhibition at the Crystal Palace.

Orchestra: Fanfare

FX: (Fade In) Crowd

PATSY HAGEN
My lords, ladies and gentlemen – we come now to the concluding round of the world's international heavyweight saxophone contest – from the Orient, with his bamboo saxophone – Fred Fumanchu!

Grams: Slight Clapping

FUMANCHU
I thank you.

PATSY HAGEN
And on my right, representing the Empire and wearing the kilt, a shamrock, four leeks and a thistle, with a turban made out of our glorious Union Jack – Major Dennis Bloodnok – an Englishman!

Grams: Furore. Cheers

PATSY HAGEN
First we will give a fair hearing to Mr Fred Fumanchu.

FUMANCHU
I thank you. (*Clears throat*)

Orchestra: 'Valse Vanité' (Last 8 Bars)

Silence

PATSY HAGEN
And now we will hear from the British contender – Major Bloodnok!

Grams: Vast Cheers

BLOODNOK
Thank you. (*Clears throat*)

Orchestra: One Note

PATSY HAGEN
The Winner!

Grams: Vast Cheers. Crowd Singing 'There'll always be an England'

PATSY HAGEN
Quiet! Quiet please! Quiet! By the merest chance, it so happens that Major Bloodnok's name is already engraved on this magnificent silver cup.

Grams: Swamp With Cheers

FUMANCHU
Stop – English people most dishonest! I make *terrible revenge* on white man.

Orchestra: Dramatic Chords

WALLACE
'The Fearful Revenge of Fred Fumanchu – the disappointed oriental bamboo saxophonist.' Chapter One. A Blow Is Struck.

FX: Thud

WALLACE
Oooh!

PETER
Chapter Two. Funeral Of An Announcer.

Grams: Fast Funeral March (Fade)

HARRY
Chapter Three.

WALLACE
The scene is in Outer Mongolia where within a life-sized reproduction of the Kremlin, three sinister figures are stooping over a hellish brew in a magnificently-equipped laboratory.

Grams: Bubbling

FUMANCHU (*raging*)
Oh boy! You see this liquid here? It will bling just retlibution on all white men for foul tlick prayed on me at Clystal Parrace Exposition. Anybody dlinking one dlop on this liquid will immediately explode anything he points at. Oh! Hot Diggoty! We have plenty fun.

HARRY (*Chinese*)
But how are we going to get fatal liquid dlunk by stupid white man?

FUMANCHU
Simple. Put in whiskey bottle and leave in Hyde Park.

WALLACE
Six months later –

Orchestra: Passage of Time

BLOODNOK
Ah! Here I am, six months later, in Hyde Park. And see! Someone has put a naughty bottle of whiskey by my ancestral home – i.e. the dustbin. Any questions? And aaah! Unless I am much mistaken, I am about to open the bottle.

FX: Bottle – Pop

BLOODNOK
Thank you. (*Gulps*) Ah! That's better.

FX: Slight Explosion

BLOODNOK
Manners!

FUMANCHU
Pardon me, please.

BLOODNOK
What do you want, you fiendish yellow devil carrying a bamboo saxophone? Are you one of those Boxer villains?

FUMANCHU
Pardon?

BLOODNOK
Have you never heard of the Boxer Rising?

FUMANCHU
Only after a count of ten.

BLOODNOK
I don't wish to know that.

FUMANCHU
Kind fliend, will do honolable favour, please?

BLOODNOK
What do you want me to do? How much? Anything for money. Here's the advertisement I put in the paper. See – 'Wanted – Money! No reasonable offer refused'.

FUMANCHU
Now, please. Here five shilling. Point finger at policeman over there.

BLOODNOK
Right.

Grams: Explosion

BLOODNOK
Good heavens, I've exploded a constabule. I've never known a copper go so far. What does this mean?

FUMANCHU
It mean you will point at everything I tell you and poof!

BLOODNOK
I won't do it. You'll have to force me.

FUMANCHU
What with?

BLOODNOK
Money.

FUMANCHU
Very well. But you are my plisoner. Only *I* can remove your fatal power. Raise hands and ears above head, please, and follow me. (*Goes off*)

BLOODNOK
You've got me. (*Aside*) But don't worry, listeners, I will secretly type a help note and leave it with a life-like oil-portrait of this yellow fiend underneath a convenient stone along with this recording of Max Geldray. There.

Max & Orchestra: 'Exactly Like You'

WALLACE
'The Dreadful Revenge of. . .' Er. . . um. . . that fellow – you know, that chap with the explodable finger . . . what's his name . . . er . . . I'll get it in a minute. Don't go away . . . (*hums and haws*).

PETER (*close to mike*)
I'd like to tell listeners now that Mr Greenslade is the *only* BBC announcer not so far approached by commercial television.

WALLACE
I've got it! 'Fred Fumanchu', Part Two.

NED
That night I was in my office at Scotland Yard listening to the commercial telly with the picture turned down.

On Disc: Ellington (distorted): We interrupt this advertisement to give police message. Scotland Yard anxious to contact man with explodable finger accompanied by sinister Chinaman who have already blown up 27,000 metal saxophones. Birmingham 4, Arsenal 0.

FX: Click

NED
Sergeant!

THROAT
Yes?

The Goons with Wallace Greenslade

NED
This is terrible! Birmingham 4, Arsenal 0, and that dreadful Chinese saxophone destroyer! My honour as Chief Commissioner depends upon his instant apprehension. By heavens! I'll offer a thousand pounds for –

MORIARTY
A thousand pounds for what?

THYNNE
Let me do the talking, Moriarty . . . Our card.

NED
What's this? 'Grytpype-Thynne and Moriarty – Eiffel Tower Specialists'? That's no good to me. I want men to track down a saxophone exploder.

THYNNE
Exactly. These Eiffel Towers are just a disguise. Moriarty, take off your Eiffel Tower. There – you can see underneath he's wearing his anti-saxophone exploding set.

NED
The very men I want. Get Fred Fumanchu!

MORIARTY
What about the money – the money?

NED
I'll give you an advance. Here's an oil painting of a cheque for three hundred pounds.

THYNNE
Good. Moriarty, take this to the Royal Academy and cash it.

MORIARTY
Right.

FX: Whoosh

THYNNE
Back to the case. Now then, Neddie, whom do you suspect?

NED
The Referee. He was obviously on Birmingham's side. Arsenal should have been three up by. . .

THYNNE
I know that. I mean the saxophone exploder.

NED
Ah, yes. Fred Fumanchu. He's trying to finish Britain as a saxophone-playing nation.

THYNNE
Gad! That goes pretty deep. Then we've *got* to stop him. Where is this fiend?

NED
I'm told he's in the vicinity.

THYNNE
Then we must wait till he comes out.

NED
But he'll recognize us in these uniforms of plain-clothes men.

THYNNE
Then we'll disguise ourselves. I know – you put on Moriarty's Eiffel Tower and I'll walk behind in mine.

NED
But wait! If Fumanchu sees *two* Eiffel Towers together he'll know one of them is a phoney.

THYNNE
Neddie, you have a sharp mind. Two Eiffel Towers must never be seen together. Take it off and we'll use my portable Nelson's column instead. You stand on top and I'll wheel you along.

NED
But won't that be rather conspicuous?

THYNNE
Certainly not, Neddie. I'll enclose the whole thing in a cardboard replica of Charing Cross Station.

NED
To think I doubted you! Have this water-colour of a cheque for £50.

THYNNE
Thank you. Moriarty!

FX: Whoosh

MORIARTY
Yes, yes?

THYNNE
Take this to the Royal Institute of Water-Colour Painters and have it changed into woodcuts.

FX: Whoosh

THYNNE
Now, Neddie, are you on top of the column? Right! Off we go!

Fade in under the following speech:
FX: Slight Traffic

WALLACE
And so, disguised as Charing Cross Station on wheels, they moved cautiously up the Strand until they were suddenly halted at the Adelphi by a familiar voice.

BLOODNOK
Roll up! Tonight for one night only! Jim Fumanchu, amazing oriental conjurer. No relation to Fred. Seats at the box office or, at a slight reduction, from me personally.

NED (*whispers*)
Look, Grytpype – Dennis Bloodnok, the confederate of Fumanchu! Jim must be Fred in disguise. No Chinaman could have a name like Jim.

MORIARTY
Neddie! We've got him! You cover the back and we'll cover the front.

THYNNE
And that's how he got away at the side.

FX: Eight Chinese Gabbling Like Keystone Cops. Car Revved Up Fast and Away

NED
There he goes!

FX: Two Shots

MORIARTY
I think you've wounded him. Yes! Look! Here's a trail of fresh noodles.

NED
After him! Quick! Into the squad car and hold tight.

FX: Coconut Shells or Slow Record of Horse & Cart

NED
Can't you go any faster?

MORIARTY
Of course.

FX: Horse & Cart Effect Speeded Up To Fantastic Speed

NED
Stop!

FX: Stops At Once

NED
We've reached a crossroads.

MORIARTY
Wait! The trail of noodles has stopped and continues with preserved ginger.

NED
We must hurry. He's reached his last course. Which road has he taken?

MORIARTY
The one to Dewsbury.

NED
Then we haven't a moment to lose. Giddap!

FX: Horse & Cart Restarts and Speeds Up. Fade Down Under:

WALLACE
Dewsbury! That was the significant word. As Seagoon well knew, in Dewsbury resided the player-owner of the last remaining metal saxophone in England.

Fade in:
FX: Bubbling Cauldron, Continuing Under and Mixed With:

Music: Corny Hot Sax Solo: 'Yellow Rose of Texas'

FX: Terrific Steam Jet

Music: Out

MINNIE (*screams*)

CRUN
Keep it still, Min. Hold that saxophone still.

MINNIE
But it's getting hot, Henry.

CRUN
I don't care, Min. How can I get this jet of green steam up it if you jiggle about?

MINNIE
Why do I have to have a jet of green steam up my saxophone?

CRUN
I keep telling you. That naughty saxophone exploder, Fred Fumanchu, is after your saxophone and this green steam will immunize it. Now – once again. One. . . two. . .

Music: Sax Solo: 'In the Mood'

FX: Terrific Steam Jet as Before

Music: Out

MINNIE (*screams*)

CRUN
No, that's no good, Min. You were playing the wrong tune. It must be 'The Yellow Man from Texas'.

MINNIE
I'm sick of playing that one, buddy.

CRUN
Then play 'Riding on a Rainbow' and I'll put on this record of Mr Ray Ellington to accompany you.

The Ray Ellington Quartet: 'Riding on a Rainbow'

WALLACE
That was Ray Ellington of whom it has been said. Next, we present 'The Dreaded Revenge of Fred Fumanchu', Part 4. And I quote, 'Part 4'. The story up to now. By passing him twice, Seagoon managed to reach the Bannister residence ahead of the dreaded Fumanchu.

NED
Now to organise the defence. Who'll volunteer?

BLUEBOTTLE
I will, my capitain. Enter Balloonbottle, son of the regiment, with cardboard waterpistol and own water in empty lemonade bottle.

NED
Noble lad! Bluebottle – from the right – number!

BLUEBOTTLE
Sixty-three.

NED
Curse! Sixty-two deserters. Oh, if we only had some more idiots to make up the number.

ECCLES (*approaches, singing*)
Twenty tiny fingers – twenty tiny toes – and I've got 'em all.

NED
You! From the right – number!

ECCLES
One!

NED
Form fours!

FX: Squad Forms Fours

NED
Let's see them do that on television! Now, Bluebottle, take this stick of dynamite.

Milligan with Larry Stephens

BLUEBOTTLE
No, I don't like this game.

NED
Shut up!

ECCLES
Shut up!

NED
Shut up, Eccles!

ECCLES
Shut up, Eccles!

NED
Now – if you see Fumanchu come up that road, light the fuse, count scramson and throw it under his car. Understand?

ECCLES
No.

NED
Good! Farewell.

FX: Whoosh

BLUEBOTTLE
Eccles!

ECCLES
Yup?

BLUEBOTTLE
You're going to light the nice stick of dynamite, aren't you?

ECCLES
Yeah, yeah.

BLUEBOTTLE
How many have you got to count up to before it explodes?

ECCLES
Um. . . oh. . . um. . . I dunno.

BLUEBOTTLE
Well, you'd better light it and count how long it takes. Then you'll know, won't you?

ECCLES
Oh, yeah. I'll light it now.

BLUEBOTTLE
No, not yet. Wait till I get behind that tree.

FX: Whoosh

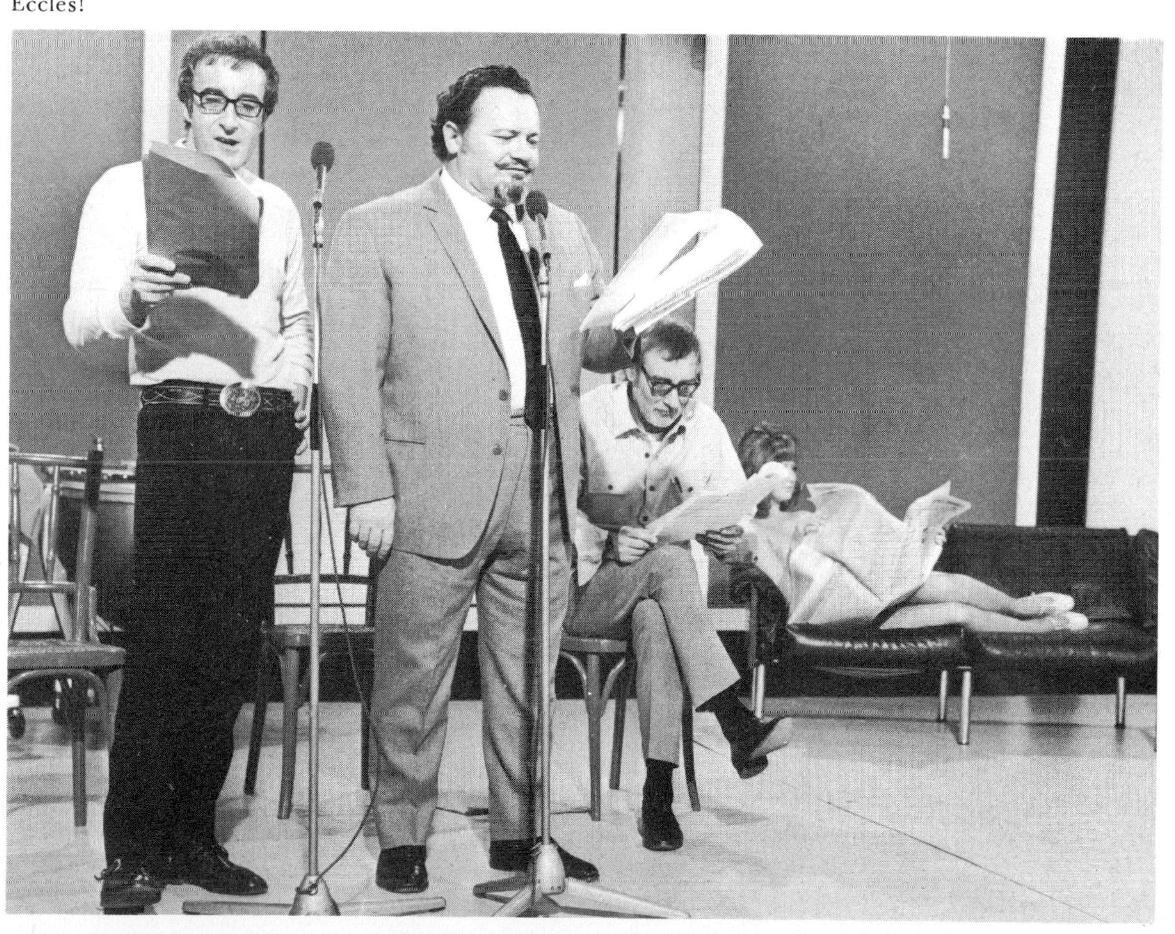

BLUEBOTTLE (*shouting, off*)
All right!

FX: Match Struck & Fizzle Continuing Under –

ECCLES
Um. . . one. . . two. . . three. . . er. . . four. . . five . . . six. . . it's getting difficult here. . . ah! . . . seven. Good job I went to High School.

BLUEBOTTLE (*off*)
What are you waiting for, Eccles?

ECCLES (*shouting*)
What comes after seven?

BLUEBOTTLE (*shouting, off*)
What did you say? I can't hear you.

ECCLES (*shouting*)
I said, 'What comes after seven?' Come over here and tell me.

BLUEBOTTLE (*shouting, off*)
No. You're not going to get me coming over there. You come over here. Now then, what is it?

ECCLES
Well, I –

FX: Explosion

Pause

ECCLES
Oooh! (*Calls*) Bluebottle! . . . Bluebottle! Oooh . . . what's this custard on the wall?

BLUEBOTTLE
Don't you touch me, you rotten swine. Scrape me off and take me home.

NED
Keep quiet, you two. I'm just about to knock at the Minnie Bannister Home for Part 5 of the Fearful Fumanchu Story.

FX: Knocking On Door

MINNIE (*off*)
Who's there?

NED
It's me.

MINNIE (*off*)
Henry, there's a man called 'Me' at the door.

CRUN (*off*)
Me? He'll have to prove it. (*Raises voice*) You, out there!

NED
Yes?

CRUN (*off*)
Prove you're me.

NED
All right. I'm Henry Crun.

CRUN (*off*)
That's me. Minnie, open the door and let me in.

MINNIE
But you *are* in, Henry.

CRUN (*off*)
Well, you'll have to let me *out*.

MINNIE (*off*)
Why?

CRUN (*off*)
Because I'm out there waiting to come in.

MINNIE (*off*)
Oh, very well.

FX: Door Opens

NED
Ah, thank you.

FX: Door Closes

Pause

NED
Now then, Mr Crun, I want to warn you that –

FX: Knocking

CRUN
Who's that out there?

MINNIE (*off*)
It's *me*. You've locked me out.

CRUN
Nonsense. *Me* just came in. He's here now.

MINNIE (*off*)
No, no, it's me – Minnie.

NED
Good heavens! Quick! That's the woman I'm here to protect. Open the door.

CRUN
Very well. But I must let Minnie in first.

FX: Door Opens

MINNIE
Thank you, Henry.

CRUN
That's all right, Minnie. Now Min — what were you —

FX: Knocking

CRUN
Who's there?

NED (*off*)
It's me. She isn't *here.*

CRUN
Rubbish. She *is* here, aren't you, Min?

MINNIE
Yes, I'm here, Henry.

NED (*off*)
Well, you're not out *here.*

MINNIE
Are you sure?

NED (*off*)
Yes. Come out and have a look.

FX: Door Opens

MINNIE
You're right. I'm not. Help! I'm lost! We'll all be murdered in our beds. (*Goes on having hysterics*)

Music: (In Distance) 'Valse Vanité' on Sax

NED
Listen! That's Fred Fumanchu playing his dreaded oriental bamboo saxophone and the swine is playing in a different key.

MORIARTY
Quick! We must fly. He's closing in from all directions.

FX: Door Bursts Open

BLOODNOK
Aiaough! Don't move, anyone! I've got you covered!

NED
Bloodnok! You treacherous renegade!

BLOODNOK
This is no time for compliments. Where's that last English saxophone? Come on!

MINNIE
I won't do it.

BLOODNOK
Why! It's Minnie — Minnie Bannister, the darling of Roper's Light Horse! Also the darling of his heavy one.

MINNIE
Oh, Dennis!

BLOODNOK
Darling, dance with me.

Music: Fast 'Blue Danube'

BLOODNOK & MINNIE (*both in ecstasy*)

NED
Stop this, you crazy Sabrina and Michael Wilding!

Music: Stops

BLOODNOK
Yes, I was forgetting my duty to friend Fumanchu. Where's the saxophone? I intend to destroy it with my explodable finger.

ECCLES
You'll do that over my dead body.

FX: Explosion

BLOODNOK
That's *that* settled!

NED
Bloodnok, you've killed the noble Eccles!

BLOODNOK
Well?

ECCLES
Yeah! Well done!

NED
Shut up, Eccles!

ECCLES
Shut up, Eccles.

BLOODNOK
Enough of these pleasantries. Where's that saxophone? Fumanchu promised me £10 to destroy it.

NED
I'll give you fifteen to join *us.*

BLOODNOK
That swine Fumanchu can't buy *me* with money.

NED
Oh, noble Englishman!

BLOODNOK
Never mind that. Where's the cash?

FX: Cash Register

BLOODNOK
And there's your receipt.

FX: Door Bursts Open

FUMANCHU
Ah! Fiendish Brudnock, you have betlayed me. I point exprodable finger at you. Take that!

FX: Explosion

NED
Gad! He's got Bloodnok

FX: Three Quick Explosions in Succession

FUMANCHU
There! Have destloyed evellybody except you, Misters Seagoon and Glytpype-Thynne.

NED
No, no! Spare our lives and I'll give you the last metal saxophone to destroy.

FUMANCHU
Oh boy! Now I will be champion bamboo saxophonist of Universe.

FX: Typing

NED
As he spoke, I surreptitiously typed a short note to Grytpype-Thynne and posted it.

THYNNE (*opening letter*)
Oh, listen, Neddie – a letter from you. 'Dear Grytpype, while I engage this bamboo saxophonist in mortal conversation, slip round under his kimono and bore a few holes in his bamboo saxophone.'

FUMANCHU
No so loud – I can hear you.

THYNNE
I'm sorry. (*Quietly*) 'P.S. Don't let him hear you reading this letter or it will mean certain death for both of us.'

FX: Two Explosions

WALLACE (*quickly*)
And, by George, he was right. Tickets are now on sale in the foyer for tonight's recital by Fred Fumanchu, the world's *only* bamboo saxophonist. I thank you.

Music: 'Valse Vanité' – Fade Under –

WALLACE
All complaints about the Goon Show should be addressed to 'Life with the Lyons', Alexandra Palace, West Croydon. Goodnight.

FX: Explosion

FUMANCHU
Oh boy! I got him, too.

Orchestra: Signature Tune

Ray Ellington

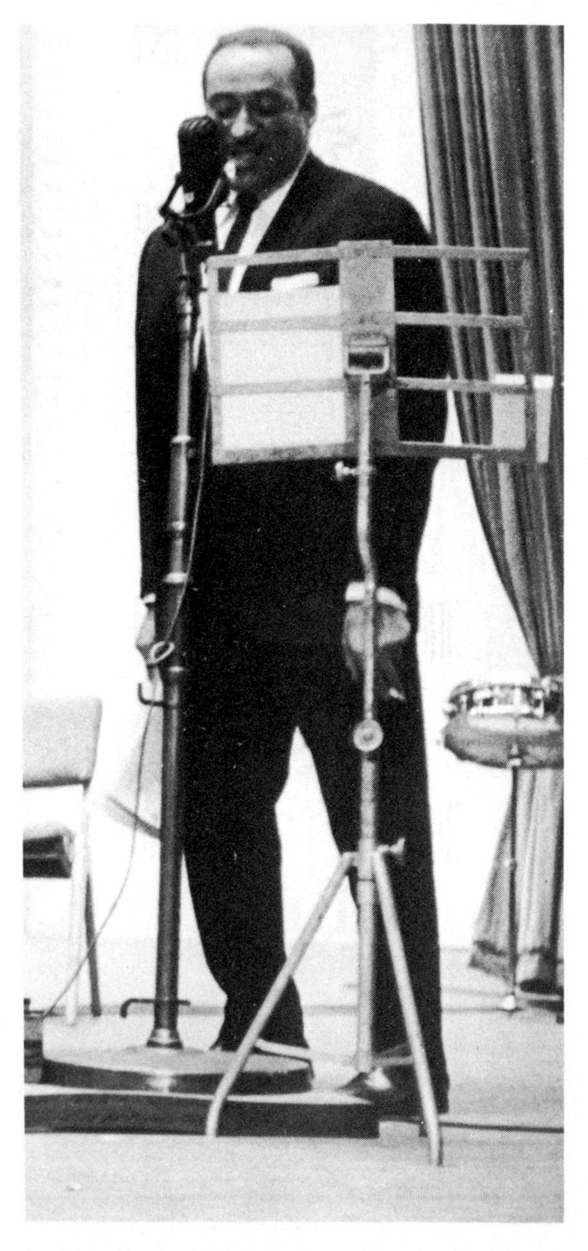

(Series 8)
Transmission: Monday, 13 January 1958
Studio: The Camden Theatre, London

CAST

Spike Milligan
Moriarty
Minnie Bannister
Spriggs
Eccles
Singhiz Lalkaka

Peter Sellers
Grytpype-Thynne
Henry Crun
Constable Mate
Major Dennis Bloodnok
Timmy Bluebottle
Mr Banajee

Harry Secombe
Inspector Neddie Seagoon

George Chisholm (Special Guest)
George

With The Ray Ellington Quartet, Max Geldray,
and the Orchestra conducted by Wally Stott.
Script by Spike Milligan.
Announcer Wallace Greenslade.
Producer Tom Ronald.

WALLACE
This is the BBC Home Service. Ladies and gentlemen, by the power of electricity and microphone placed in the proximity of the protagonists, we present an all wireless show, with a brandy base.

Grams: Commercial Disc (Old) Jack Hylton. Fade Away

HARRY
That music should give you a clue to the financial position of the BBC's Music Department.

SPIKE (*angry*)
One moment, Mr Secombe, you can't attack the Corporation from the back.

HARRY
Can't I? Bend down!

FX: Slapstick

HARRY
Right in his old lunch. Now read the name of the play.

WALLACE
We present 'The Great String Robberies'.

Orchestra: Dramatic Theme (Not Blaring – Mysterious)

PETER
The string robberies started very simply with a man saying

MORIARTY
My socks keep coming down.

THYNNE
Oh? Say 'Ahh'.

MORIARTY
Ahhhhhh.

THYNNE
Gad, you've got hoar-frost on the ankle.

MORIARTY
Is that dangerous?

THYNNE
If it kills you, *yes*.

MORIARTY
Owwwwww owwwwww!

THYNNE
Owwwwing won't help.

MORIARTY
I'm dying. I must get elastic for my socks.

THYNNE
No, there's a waiting list for that. We must try and obtain a certain amount of cheap string.

MORIARTY
What do I do till then?

THYNNE
For the time being you keep your socks up with the famous Eccles method.

MORIARTY
What's that?

THYNNE
Stand on your head –

FX: Temple Block

THYNNE
There. Now put these skates under your head, and off you go.

Grams: Roller Skating On Pavements or Wood, Whichever Sounds Best

MORIARTY (*yells*)

Orchestra: Three Dramatic Chords. . . Soft

NED (*megaphone*)
Hello folks! Three days later, I was called from Scotland Yard to Scotland. At Edinburgh Station I was met by a platform.

Grams: Train Standing In the Station Whistles & Gives Off a Great Fast Jet of Steam

PETER (*Flowerdew*)
Screeammm! Ohh, there should be a law against trains letting off steam when people are wearing kilts.

NED
Excuse me, porter. I'm a stranger here, could you tell me the way to walk?

PETER (*all sad*)
Aye. You see yon ticket barrier? Well, head for that.

NED
Thank you.

GEORGE
Inspector Seagoon?

NED
The voice came from underneath a red navy kilt.

Impressions of Archbishop Makarios during EOKA week in Camden Town, 1955: Milligan with Eric Sykes

GEORGE
Aye. I'm a ventriloquist I throw ma voice, sometimes from ma knee, sometimes from ma shin and sometimes (*pinch nose*) from ma nose.

NED (*pinching nose*)
Jolly good. Now, where's the scene of the crime?

GEORGE
I'll take you there. Here, hold this steering wheel and make this noise: Brbbbrrrbbb (*motor car*).

NED
Brrrrrrrrrrrrrr. (*Both fade off*)

Cross Fade

NED & GEORGE (*approaching*)
Brrrrrrrrr.

GEORGE
This is the hoose.

PETER
Aye, welcome to the scene of the crime.

NED
Er. . . where's the front door?

PETER
In this brown paper parcel.

FX: Unwrapping of Paper

PETER
We only use it for going in and out. Aaaah – there.

FX: Door Opens

PETER
The black-bearded criminal must have got in through the door or windows – everything else was locked.

NED
Right. Now, who was killed?

PETER
No one's been killed.

NED
Then this is a job for the police.

PETER
You *are* a policeman.

NED
Yes, I wasted no time getting here. Hands up, you're all under arrest.

PETER
We've done nutting.

NED
Wasting my time, eh? What are you hiding? Come on, out with it.

PETER
Not in this weather, surr!

FX: Door Opens

WALLACE
'The String Robberies', Part Two.

FX: Door Closes

NED
Part Two? That's us!!

PETER
You see that piece of string on the table?

NED
Yes, what's that space in the middle?

PETER
That's the piece that's missing.

NED
So *that's* what a piece of missing string looks like. Where's it gone? Ahh, but wait, can't you see, poor Scottish fools, it's all a practical joke! Someone's cut that string in the centre, and pulled the two pieces in opposite directions, giving the impression that a piece has been removed from the middle.

PETER
Hairy Gringlers – he's right! If you put these two pieces together, the gap disappears.

GEORGE
Aye, but did you notice when you did that the two outside ends got shorter?

NED
Gad, yes – that's it. Now I see what happened. What cunning! The criminal cut a piece off each end, *then* cut across the middle, and pulled them apart, making the string look the original length.

PETER
Oh, dear – this makes it a baffling case.

NED
Yes, instead of one piece, we're looking for two separate ends. It's a good job I can count. We must start investigations.

Orchestra: Link

WALLACE (*distorted pre-recording*)
Finally, here is a police message. Will all people in possession of two pieces of string please report to their local police station. Now, Sport. The

boxing match between the Irish and Italian Football teams has been cancelled as . . . *(fades himself).*

CRUN
Oh dear. . . oh dearrr. (*Calls*) Min?? Min??

MINNIE
Yes?

CRUN
Hurry up – I'm next.

MINNIE (*off*)
I haven't finished yet.

CRUN
Oh, that sinful woman, always at the cigarette-rolling machine.

MINNIE
Got a match, Henery?

CRUN (*goes into heart attack*)
Ohhh grarph!!! You vixen, not satisfied with making your own fags, now you want to smoke them!

MINNIE
Ah, but this is herbal tobacco made from wild dandelions.

CRUN
Well, don't you leave any in my bedroom. Our water rates are high enough as it is, Min.

MINNIE
Henery, how do you like my new frock?

CRUN (*horrors*)
Min, Min. . . Where did you get that sack dress?

MINNIE
I got if off the coalman.

CRUN
You mean he's walking around naked?

MINNIE
Yes, that's why his prices are so high.

CRUN
I'll talk to you about this later, Miss Bannister. Right now, we go to the police station about string!

MINNIE
No, Henery, you're not allowed out – so you sit by the fire and I'll drive the house there.

Grams: Old Car Banging & Honking Away Into Distance. Yells & Screams From Both

WALLACE
As the house drives away, we arrive at 'The String Robberies', Part three.

NED (*megaphone*)
Hello folks, calling all folks! Three weeks, and still no nearer solving the crime. I think I'll have a bath.

FX: Sandpapering Sound. Loud Heavy Coarse Sandpaper

NED
Ah, there's nothing like a bit of sandpaper for bringing the old knees up white.

MATE
Errr, pardon me, Inspector.

NED
Constable Mate, how dare you creep in here when my shins are exposed.

MATE
Sorry, I won't look, Inspector. Any case, I'm a married man with shins of me own.

NED (*impatient*)
Constable, state your business.

MATE
I'm a polistman.

NED
I know. What do you want?

MATE
Well, dere's an 'ouse outside to see you.

NED
House? Male or female?

MATE
I couldn't tell, it had the blinds drawn, mate.

NED
I must go and inspect it. Meantime, Max Geldray will show what fun can be had with an ordinary pair of woollen drawers and a pair of thin legs. Brandy!

Max & Orchestra: Music

Orchestra: Few Return-to-Story Chords

FX: Knocking on door from out of Music. Door Opens

NED
Good morning. I was told that this house wanted to see me.

CRUN
Ah sir, we have come to hand in our three pieces of string.

NED
Must be some mistake, we only wanted people with two pieces.

CRUN
Oh, then I'll throw one piece away.

NED
Good, now you're a suspect! (*Aside*) Hello folks, I wonder – could this aged man be the string thief?

CRUN
No sir.

NED
Shhh – not so loud – he might hear.

MINNIE
Put your fingers in your ears, Henery.

CRUN
Oh, all right.

Pause

NED
. . . the robberies been done –

Pause

NED
. . . never will be a sol –

Pause

MINNIE
. . . there was much of a –

Pause

MINNIE
– and comes home roaring –

Pause

NED
What I . . . it cou . . . can't ge . . . (*continues to ad lib behind* –)

WALLACE
Dear listeners, this disjointed conversation is being caused by Mr Crun moving his fingers in and out of his ears, thereby causing an intermittent break in sound.

CRUN
It's all in my mind, you know.

NED
By your shape it looks as if it's all in your trousers.

CRUN
Steady, sir, I may be seventy-nine but I have the strength of a man of ninety-two.

NED
Mr Crun, I must warn you to keep the peace.

CRUN
What piece? Don't worry about us keeping the peace, tell that Foster Dulles idiot.

MINNIE
Come, Henery, before he endorses your provisional dandruff licence.

Grams: Car Drives Away As Before. Bangs etc. Minnie and Crun (Pre-recorded) Singing. Fade

NED
Constable! Follow that house

Grams: Running Footsteps. Over them, Mate's voice (pre-recorded) 'Come back House – I arrest you in the name of the law'

NED
Throw a cordon round England – no one must leave the island!

Orchestra: Three short chords. Dramatic – Not too Loud

WALLACE
'The String Robberies', Part Thrune. The Scene – the Cliffs of Dover.

Grams: Seagulls

MORIARTY
Grytpype, they've spotted us.

THYNNE
It'll brush off.

MORIARTY
In the paper it says there is a nation-wide search for people with two pieces of string.

THYNNE
We must leave England! Bring the brown paper pudding, and follow me. Hup!

Grams: Splash Splash

THYNNE
I suspected it, Moriarty, I suspected it all the time – the English Channel's made entirely of water.

MORIARTY
Oh, what luck – I'll put some in a bottle in case we get thirsty.

THYNNE
Head for the French coast.

MORIARTY
My feet can touch bottom.

THYNNE
You must be deformed.

MORIARTY
I can't seem to get away from the shore. (*Struggles*)

THYNNE
Neither can I – England must be swimming after us. Here, swallow these condition powders.

BOTH (*Gulp*)

Grams: Burst Of A Motor Boat Going Away At Speed. Plus Screams of Grytpype-Thynne and Moriarty

THYNNE
Hold on, Moriarty.

MORIARTY
Oooh, the power at last, the power!

THYNNE
Keep it aft.

WALLACE
Meantime, a hundred miles away, Seagoon springs from a foreign bed.

NED
Hup!

FX: Doingg. Duck Call

NED
Aaahhh! As I jumped out of bed I thought I heard two splashes.

SPRIGGS
Are your feet wet? Are your feet wet, Jiimmmmm?

NED
Yes, I've been sleeping with damp socks on.

SPRIGGS
Can't you afford a clothes-line, Jim?

NED
Yes, but I find a bed more comfortable.

SPRIGGS
Oh Jim, we must take action, Jiimmmmm.

NED
Right, Jiimmmmm, send a signal to –

Grams: Naval Morse Code Electronic Signal, High-Pitched

NED
All coast guards, especially those on the coast, arrest the owners of those splashes.

Orchestra: Bloodnok Link

Grams: Great Heavy Waves Pounding The Shore. Pebbles Being Hurled Up & Down Beach. Wind Howling

BLOODNOK
Ohhhh. . . Hhhhh . . . Ohhhh. . . I've never had it as bad as this. Oh, the wind must be forty knots. I hope we don't have to launch the lifeboat tonight. Just in case they ask me I'll just put one arm in a sling, and lie down in a mock faint.

FX: Knock On Door

BLOODNOK
Who's that? Only a lunatic would be out in such a storm.

FX: Doop Opens

BLOODNOK
Yes?

ECCLES (*ahem*)
Good King Wenceslas looked out on der feast of Stephen, when the snow lay all about, deep and crisp and even. Brightly shone the moon dat night tho' the frost was cruel, when an old man came in sight, gathering winter feeeeeuuuuuullllll.

Grams: Pre-Record Eccles About Six Times to Give the Effect of a Choir of Eccleses. In the Studio Spike Will Sing Live to Add the Effect of Depth

BLOODNOK
Thank you

FX: Door Slams. Knocking On Door. Door Opens

BLOODNOK
Yes?

ECCLES
Merry Christmas.

FX: Shaking a Wooden Collecting Box

BLOODNOK
You crazy mixed-up Eccles! Christmas has gone.

ECCLES
Which way did it go?

BLOODNOK
It's finished.

ECCLES
Ohhh . . . er . . . ohhhh . . . (*muttering*) Penny fer the Guy.

FX: Wooden Money Box Rattled

BLOODNOK
That's not till next November.

ECCLES
Can we come in and wait?

FX: Slapstick and Wallops

Grams: Eccles Shouting 'Ohs' & 'Ahs'

FX: Door Slams

BLOODNOK
Oh, that's got rid of those idiots.

FX: Knock on Door

BLOODNOK
Where's that club?

FX: Door Opens. Renewed Clubbing – Slapstick – Thuds

BLOODNOK (*over*)
Take that and that and that . . .

SPRIGGS
Thank you, Jim.

BLOODNOK
Ooohhh, I'm sorry, I didn't recognize you under that rain of blows.

SPRIGGS
I don't recognize myself, now. I don't like clubbing, Jim . . . I don't like it at all. I have a message for you, Jim.

BLOODNOK
Play it on the gramophone.

Grams: Typing

BLOODNOK
Curse, it's written in typewriter and I can't speak a word of it. What's on the other side?

Grams: Pre-Recording of Ten Eccleses Singing 'Good King Wenceslas'

BLOODNOK
Oh, this is too much. Ellington, attack the hit parade with a melody divine. Brandy!!

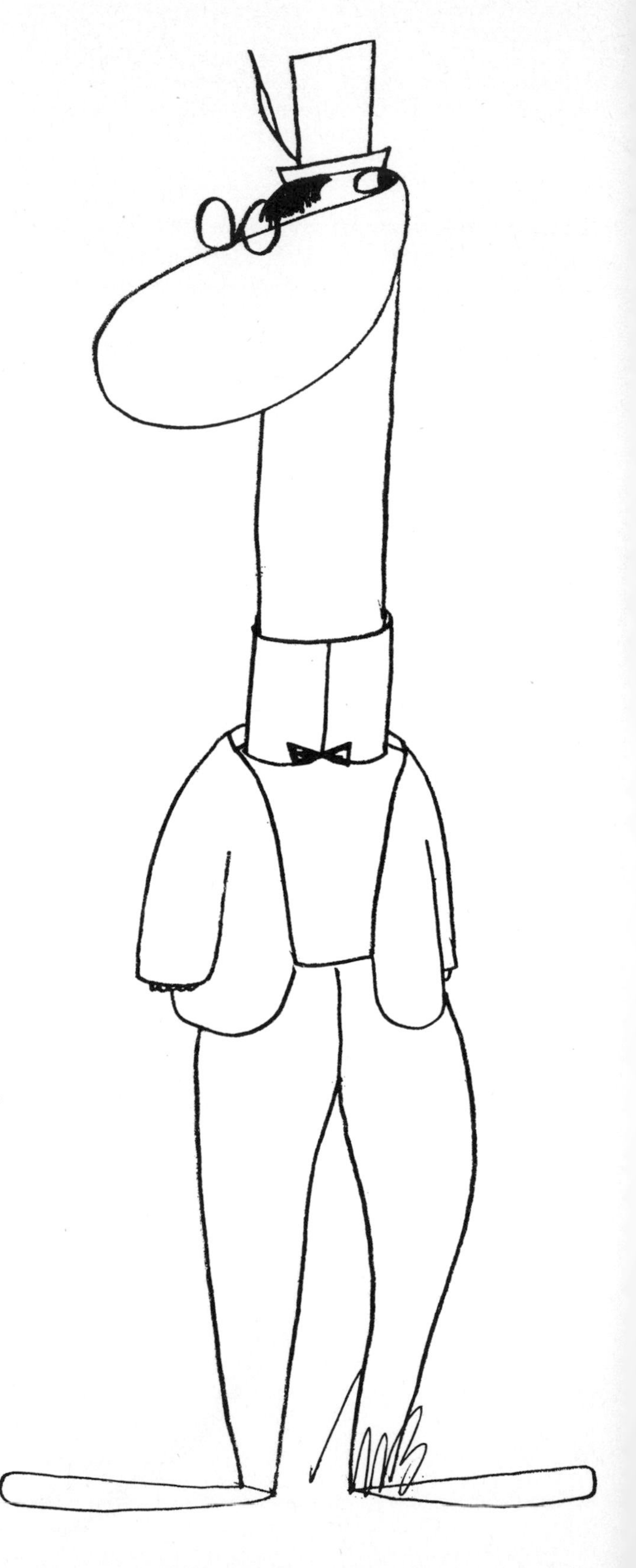

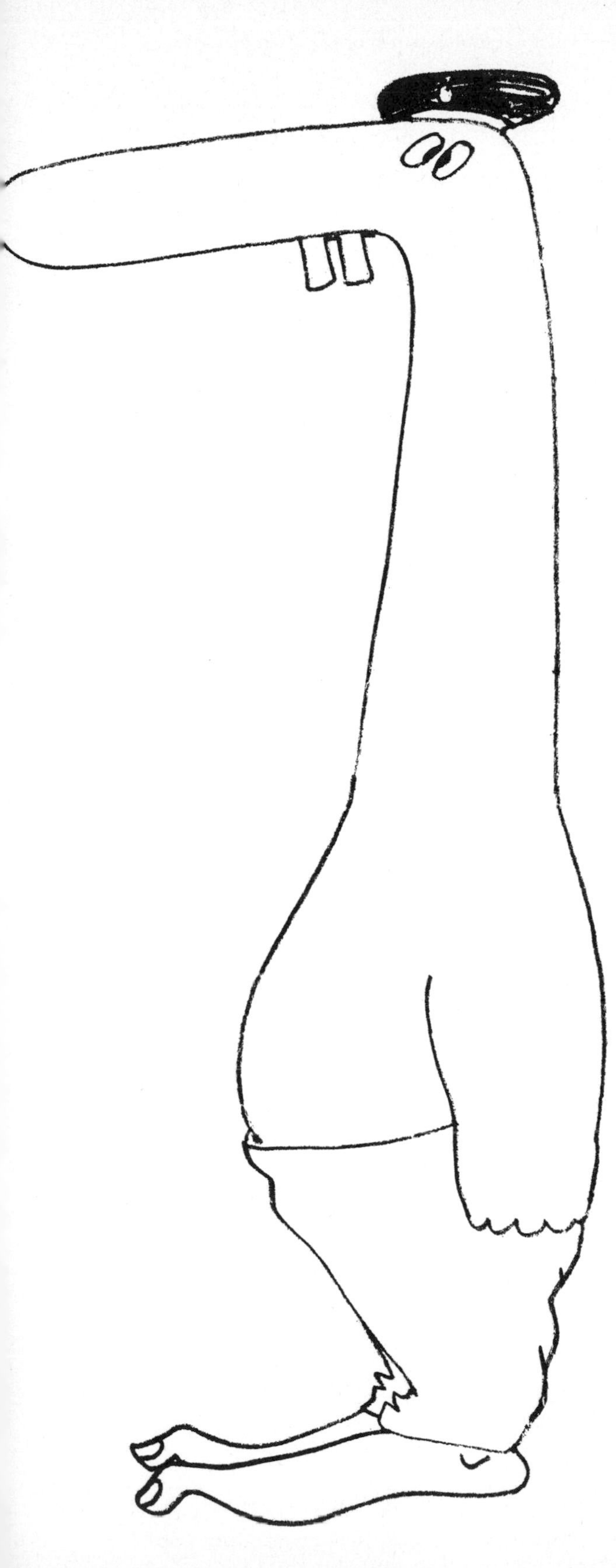

Grams: Great Running Away Of Boots – Screams etc.

The Ray Ellington Quartet: Music

WALLACE
That was Ray Ellington. We all wish him a speedy recovery. Now, by clenching my fists, gritting my teeth and contracting my abdomen, I find myself in an ideal position to hear Part Three of 'The String Robberies'.

Orchestra: Soft Mysterious Dramatic Chords

Grams: Storm At Sea. Ships' Timbers Groaning

NED
It was very brave of you to put the lifeboat out in this storm.

BLOODNOK
Yes, it's amazing what a man will do at pistol-point.

NED
What's our position?

BLOODNOK
I don't really know, I'm a stranger round here.

NED
What's the label on this wave say? Made in Birmingham for the English Channel.

MORIARTY (*off*)
Helppppppppp!

NED
Look, I can see the word coming out of the thinks-type bubble.

BLOODNOK
It must be a drowning cartoonist. (*Calls*) Here, catch this pencil and paper!

MORIARTY
Merci, I'll draw a life-belt. Ahhhh, there – saved! Now I'll draw myself on board. . . Touché.

THYNNE (*sotto*)
I'll do the talking, Moriarty.

MORIARTY
Right, I'll do the splits.

FX: Tearing of Trousers (Or, For the Prudish – Socks)

MORIARTY
Help! The sea's getting in.

THYNNE
Bend down while I bail you out.

Grams: Bailing Out Sounds

NED
All night long we bailed out Moriarty's water-logged trousers, and by dawn we could see the bottom of his boots.

THYNNE
It was a near thing for the dear Count.

NED
Perhaps now you'd like to answer a few questions.

MORIARTY
Certainement.

NED
First I must ask you to empty your pockets.

FX: Great Series of Assorted Sounds. Forks, Spoons, Odd Coins, Tubular Bells, Rocks, Stones, Small Bells, Rings, Wooden Clogs, Empty Fish Tins, Half A Pound of Gravel, Motor Horn, Pop, Alarm Clock, Whistle, etc.

NED
Quit stalling – empty your pockets.

THYNNE
Sir – that's our entire worldly wealth.

NED
What's the ominous bulge in the seat of your trousers?

MORIARTY (*furious*)
It's nothing, I tell you, just some old clothes.

NED
We'll soon see – Bloodnok, hand me that stick.

FX: Colossal Slap

BLUEBOTTLE
Owwwwww . . . my lughole!

NED
Gad – a stowaway. Come on out.

BLUEBOTTLE
All right, I'll come out. Lowers flap of Moriarty's trousers. Steps out – waits for audience applause.

Applause

BLUEBOTTLE
Not enough, I say. Puts on own clapping.

Grams: Ovation, Whistles, Cheers, Cries of Encore

NED
Stop! Who are you?

BLUEBOTTLE
I'm young Timmy Bluebottle, Ace Private Detective. Own catapult, own scooter, own legs. Will go anywhere in Finchley.

NED
Lad, lad, little loony lad, who were you trailing?

BLUEBOTTLE
I'm after the string criminals. I suspect the Moriarty man. Points finger. Point – point – pointeeeeeee.

MORIARTY
Lies, lies, all lies.

BLUEBOTTLE
Keep him away from me! Lets fly with catapult – ping!

Grams: Shattering of Shop-Front Plate Glass Window

MORIARTY
Owwwwww, my spectacles.

NED
All right, gentlemen – a final question. Are you the owner of these splashes?

Grams: Two Fast Splashes

THYNNE
No, I've never seen those splashes before in my life.

NED
Would you care to try them on?

MORIARTY
If you wish.

Grams: Two Splashes

BLUEBOTTLE
There, dey fit dem perfectly. Arrest them in the nim of law.

MORIARTY
Run for it!

Grams: Few Short Departing Fast Steps. Two Fast Splashes

NED
They've escaped with the two splashes. After them!

Grams: Thundering of Feet Followed By Four Fast Splashes

LITTLE JIM
They've fallen in the water!

Orchestra: Dramatic Soft Mysterious Chords

NED (*megaphone*)
Hello folks, this is the position to date. Moriarty and Grytpype have landed at Dover disguised as splashes and are making inland. They thumb a lift from a passing house.

Grams: Old Car (As Before) Stopping

CRUN
How far are you going, sir?

MORIARTY
Are you going anywhere near the New Forest?

CRUN
No.

MORIARTY
That suits us fine.

FX: Door Closes

CRUN
Off you go, Min.

MINNIE
We'll have to stop at the next builder's yard — we're very low on bricks.

CRUN
Funny, this house has always done thirty bricks to the mile.

Grams: Old Car Drives Away. Banging & Popping. Approach Of A Crowd of Men Running to a Stop

NED (*breathless*)
Curses — they drove away in that house.

BLUEBOTTLE
Don't worry, Captain, I took a photograph of the number.

NED
Good lad. And what luck — here comes a Hindu photographer's dark room.

Grams: Car Pulls to A Hurried Stop

FX: Knock. Door Opens

SINGHIZ
You were knocking on the door, is that correct?

NED
We want this camera developed.

SINGHIZ
Ready in a few moments. If you will accommodate yourself.

FX: Closes Door

SINGHIZ
Mr Banajee?

BANAJEE
What are you calling my name for, Mr Lalkaka?

SINGHIZ
I thought it might be attached to you, man. We have had sudden employment, in the nature of developing a film.

BANAJEE
Ah, this has come at a most obsense moment. I was in the intrepid process of wrapping up the curry powder.

SINGHIZ
You will have to postpone the making of curry for the temporary moment.

BANAJEE
It will be difficult, but I understand the necessary of gainful employment, therefore I am willing to concur.

SINGHIZ
Abka dhost. Then will you please place the European-type film in the developer tray for preparation.

BANAJEE
Eck dum. (*For the foul-minded this means 'at once'*)

FX: General Tinkling Sounds of Moving Developing Trays

SINGHIZ & BANAJEE
(*moving backwards and forwards at all times, discussing the merits of film developing*)

FX: Tapping on Door

NED
Hurry in there, you Babus —

FX: Door Opens

SINGHIZ
Here is the developed print.

NED
Let's see. Look — the number of the house is 66 Minger Lane! Arrest all houses with that address.

BLOODNOK
Wait — 66 Minger Lane — that's where Henry Crun lives.

NED
So, he's done the dirty on me.

BLOODNOK
It'll wash off, lad.

NED
Men, this is the plan. We go to the empty space in the street where Crun's house lives, we go down in the cellar and wait for Crun's house to arrive.

BLOODNOK
We must hurry – the audience is leaving.

Grams: Great Thunder of Feet Running Away

FX: Phone Rings in Foreground

Grams: Return of One Pair of Boots, Running

NED (*breathless*)
Hello, yes? Major Bloodnok? Hold on, I'll get him.

Grams: Footsteps Gallop Away. Pause. A Fresh Pair of Booted Feet Approaches

BLOODNOK (*exhausted*)
Yes, hello? Bloodnok here.

NED
Hurry, Major, we're all waiting up the street for you.

BLOODNOK
Thank you.

FX: Receiver on Hook

Grams: Running Boots Going Into Distance. (One Pair)

WALLACE
Those running boots are a repeat of the running boots you heard in 'Those Were The Days' on the Light Programme on March 2nd, and were taken from the BBC great sound library of 9000 scratchy records. I should at this juncture like to thank the Wallace Greenslade Fan Club, whose thirty-nine thousand members clubbed together and sent me a copy of last year's birthday honours. How nice to have such nice sweet friends.

THYNNE
He's a bit of a crawler, Moriarty.

MORIARTY
Shhhhh.

CRUN
This is as far as my house goes, gentlemen.

MORIARTY
Oh, can we stay here until it gets dark?

CRUN
Well, if you shut your eyes it gets dark right away.

MORIARTY
He's right, Grytpype.

NED
Hands up, you two men in the dark there!

THYNNE
Where are you?

NED
Under the floorboards in the cellar. Don't move or I'll fire.

BLUEBOTTLE
Captain, from where I'm lying I can see up Moriarty's trousers. He he.

NED
Let me see . . . Gad, I never knew he was so old.

MORIARTY
What do you want?

NED
Hand down the two pieces of string tied around your socks.

THYNNE
Dear listeners, as there is no audible sound for a piece of string, we substitute this.

Grams: Peter Sellers Long Mad Talking Record

NED
Moriarty, you're under arrest. Mr. Crun – how do we get up out of this cellar?

CRUN
There's no cellar in this house.

NED
No cellar? Then where are we?

CRUN
You're all in your mind . . . Ha hehehehehehe . . .

NED
Helpppp! Who wrote this script? Helppppp! Let us out! Helppppp!

Orchestra: 'Old Comrades March' (Ned shouts 'Helpppp' All Through Signature Tune)

The Spon Plague

(Series 8)
Transmission: Monday, 3 March 1958
Studio: The Camden Theatre, London

CAST

Peter Sellers
Grytpype-Thynne
Nurse
Mate
Henry Crun
Major Dennis Bloodnok
Bluebottle
Mr Lalkaka

Spike Milligan
Count Jim 'Kidney Wiper' Moriarty
Flutt
Minnie Bannister
Eccles
Spriggs
Mr Banajee

Harry Secombe
Dr Neddie Seagoon

George Chisholm (Special Guest)
A Scottish sentry

With The Ray Ellington Quartet, Max Geldray,
and the Orchestra conducted by Wally Stott.
Script by Spike Milligan.
Announcer Wallace Greenslade. Producer Charles Chilton.

WALLACE
This is the BBC Home Service. It might not sound much but (*tearfully*) it's home to me. (*Sings*) We've been together nah fer forty years and it ain't been a day . . .

FX: Pistol Shot

HARRY
Got him, folks. It was the kindest way out. We had the vet's permission. Now, folks, by permission of one of the Lord Chamberlain's secretaries, we present –

Orchestra: Timpani Roll (Come in on word 'Secretary')

SPIKE
'The Great Spon Plague.'

Orchestra: Dramatic Chords (New ones, please)

PETER
My name is Doctor Hairy MacSquirter, Squirter MacSquirters of the Clan MacThud Thud and Jim Thudder of Leeds – our history goes back over half a decade. I've got nothing to do with tonight's show, so I'll bid ye all a guid night.

Orchestra: Chord In C. Tatty À La Pit Orchestra

WALLACE
The scene opens in a granny-hurling factory in Tooting.

FX: Stone Chisel Sculpting On Granite. Then Hammering Iron From the Forge

THYNNE (*over the FX*)
Gad, it's my masterpiece! Don't move, Moriarty, keep that pose. How Michaelangelo would have envied me.

MORIARTY
What are you making?

THYNNE
A pill, Moriarty.

MORIARTY
What – Sapristi – you mean you made me pose nude as a model for a pill?

THYNNE
I wasn't using all of you, just a certain area. Just round off the pill with sandpaper.

FX: Sharp Rubbing with Sandpaper Over Above Speech

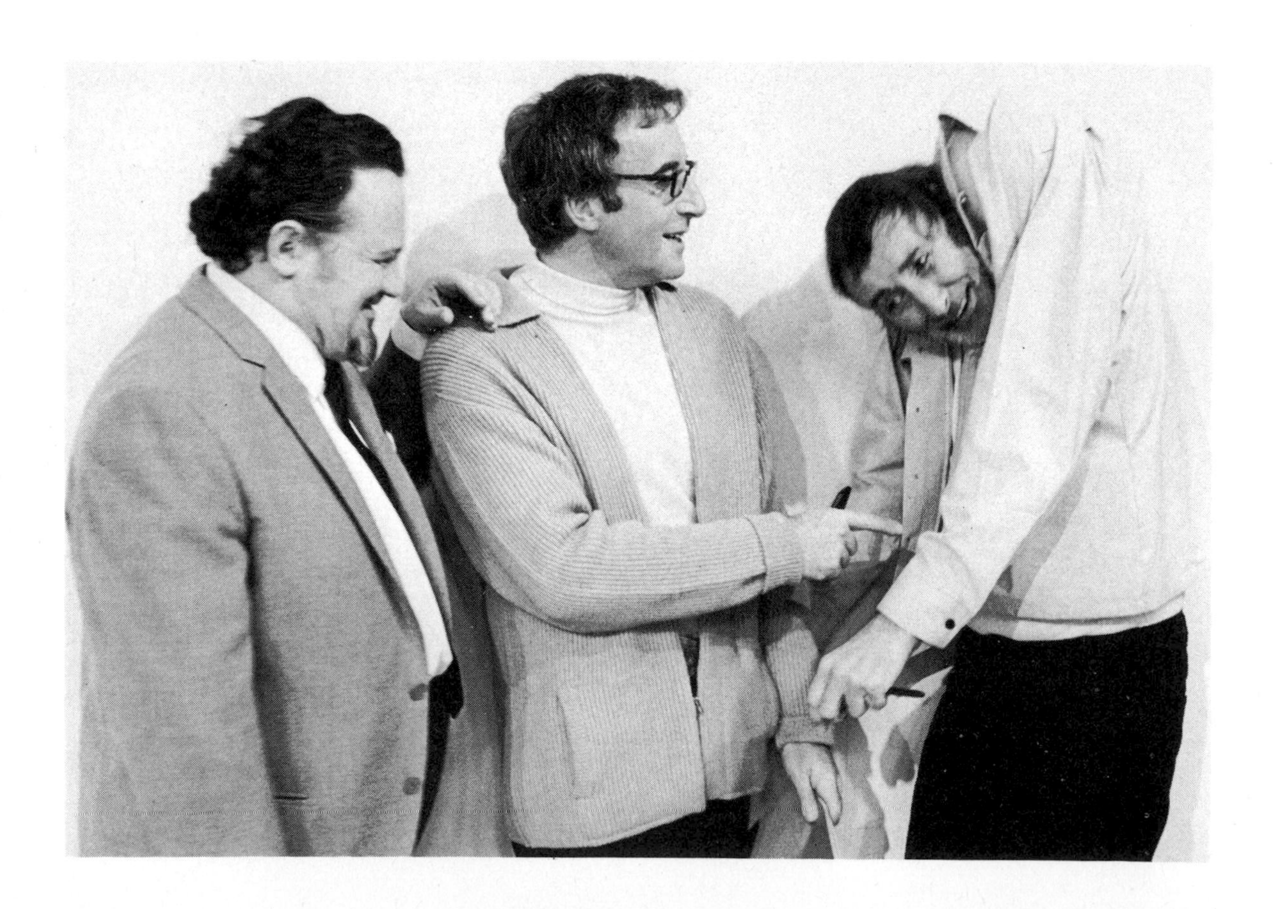

THYNNE
There – swallow it.

MORIARTY (*gulps*)
Ah, what delicious sandpaper. Banana – the flavour of the month. Owwwwwwwwww, more!

THYNNE
Listen, pay attention, you decimated, sparsely-haired French owner of a whopper. I have invented this pill to make us rich.

MORIARTY
You mustn't be too ambitious, Grytpype, we already own three pieces of brown paper and a conker.

THYNNE
Don't let that dazzle you. We must go on! Remember, 'There comes a tide in the time of every man's affairs'. You know who said that, Moriarty?

MORIARTY
You did, I just heard you. Ah, yes – Shakespeare.

THYNNE
Ignorant swine, it was Henery the Fifth, a great writer. You know the old Apollo Theatre?

MORIARTY
Yes.

THYNNE
Well, he wrote that. Now, get into this mass of chains.

FX: Chains

THYNNE (*without waiting for FX*)
Now stand on your head in this bucket of luke-warm water.

MORIARTY
Ow . . .

FX: Head In Bucket Of Water

THYNNE
Now, I pour this bottle of rancid yak butter over your knees, so. Next, hold this copy of the *Feathered World* under your nose, and fit this cricket ball under your chin. There. Next, I haul you up to the ceiling.

FX: Quick Winching when he says 'Haul Up'

MORIARTY (*slightly alarmed*)
What are you going to do now?

THYNNE
Just talk to you. Can you hear me talking?

MORIARTY
Only in words.

THYNNE
Splendid, my little thin-legged steamer. I shall use just words then.

MORIARTY
It's a miracle, I tell you.

THYNNE
This pill is the only known and unknown cure for the Spon Plague.

MORIARTY
Spon? Is it catching?

THYNNE
I don't know, no one's ever had it.

MORIARTY
You mean that yar yar yar boo the tar marg al lung tal mor pol tol nonl doll roll coll yar la backa ta la tickkiety takck a tooo?

THYNNE (*excited*)
You have it in a nutshell!

MORIARTY
But how do you know people are going to start catching the Spon Plague?

THYNNE
Leave that to me . . . I have certain arglers on the Splott mickledoooodle and the Blim blam bloo.

WALLACE
And on that beautifully enunciated rubbish we move to . . .

NED
Me, folks, Neddie!

Grams: Ovation

NED
Ta. You get all free draws for Christmas. Now for a quick bath.

Grams: Splash

NED
Now, where's that instruction manual, 'Bath Night for Beginners'? Ahhh. Take soap in right hand and apply to all parts . . . (*Fade*)

PETER (*newsreel*)
This was the great National Health Surgeon, Ned Seagoon, who has just invented dirty necks . . .

NED
La ta ta ta teeeeee . . . Flutt!

FLUTT
Yeeeeees sir?

NED
Ah, Jimmmm, stand in the sink and take a letter. First, what have I got in my diary this week?

FLUTT
Mon, Tues, Wed, Thurs, Fri and Sat.

NED
Cancel them. I can't see them till Sunday. Well, I'd better be getting down to the surgery.

Grams: Getting Out of Bath (To Go With Above Dialogue)

FX: Door Opens and Closes

Grams: Screams

FX: Door Opens In a Hurry

NED
Ha ha – I forgot my clothes!

Orchestra: Short Link, Very Weird Notes All Over The Place. Unfinished Cadences, Melody Passes From Instrument to Instrument With a Key Change At the Same Time

WALLACE
The scene: Dr Seagoon's National Health waiting-room.

Grams: Agonized Groans, Screams. People Falling to the Floor. Occasional Snoring

FX: Door Opens

NED
Ah, good morning, patients. Sorry to be so late, but I had to stop for a three month's holiday in Paris.

NURSE
Shall I send the first patient in?

NED
Yes, darling. Remember, the rich ones first, National Healths last.

NURSE
You first – drop 'em.

MATE
Ta, nurse.

NED
Now, what's the trouble with you?

MATE
I got the Shoo Shoo.

Grams: Crows

MATE
I got a touch of the birds. Get off – shoo, birdies.

NED
Gad, crows, starlings, pigeons – you'll soon be the Man in the White Suit. Ha ha ha ha ha. Well, getting the bird is a common complaint.

MATE
Yerst, I saw you last week at Coventry. 'Ere, you do all right for fruit, don't you.

NED
It's all lies, folks, I'm a great success.

MATE
Well, how can I cure these birds, mate?

NED
Soon have you well, just wear these bird-cages hanging on your legs. And take this bird-lime three times a second.

MATE
Oh, lovely . . .

NED
Who's next?

RAY
The Ellington Quartet.

NED
What's wrong with him?

RAY
This!

The Ray Ellington Quartet: Music

WALLACE
What a terrible illness that must be. And now I have pleasure in announcing a knock at the door.

FX: A Knock

NED
I have pleasure in saying 'Come in'.

FX: Door Opens

THYNNE
Ah, dear Doctor Ned. I bring you a man stricken with a dread disease. He is Count Jim 'Kidney Wiper' –

Secombe with harmonica-player Max Geldray

FX: Swanee Whistle

THYNNE
– Moriarty.

MORIARTY
Owwww, save me, Doctor . . .

NED
Right, just lie face-down on this back. Now, just run a stethoscope over his pockets. Gad, this man is suffering from poverty. Take this bottle of pound notes and inject them into his wallet three times a day.

MORIARTY
Owwwwwwwwww . . . Lovely medicine.

THYNNE
Dear Surgeon, you have overlooked one terrifying aspect of the dear Count's condition. This man has the Spon Plague.

NED
I've never heard of it.

THYNNE
That's because the Count is the first man to have caught it.

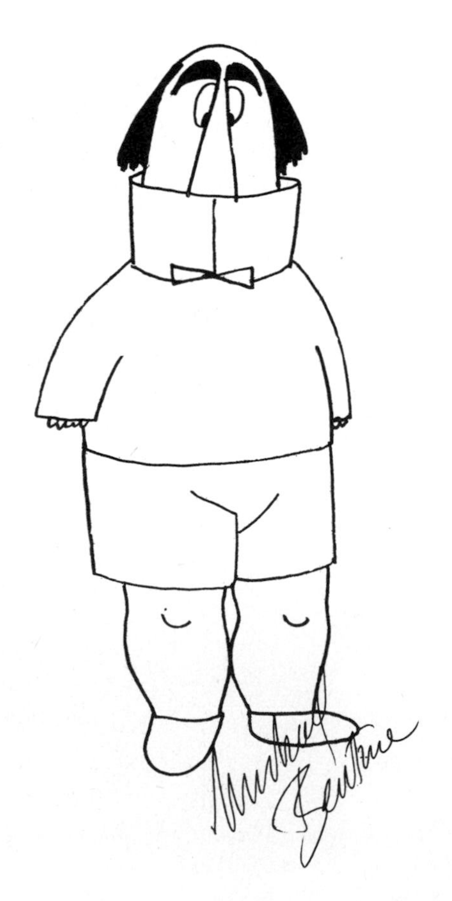

NED
Are you sure?

THYNNE
He has all the symptoms – namely, bare knees.

NED
Is it catching?

THYNNE
Yes – stand back! Too late – you've got it.

NED
What what what what what?

THYNNE
You've got the bare knees.

NED
No I haven't.

THYNNE
Roll your trousers up.

FX: Wooden Venetian Blind Pulled Up

THYNNE
There – bare knees.

NED
Ahhhhhhh – I've got the Spon!

Grams: Absolute Running At High Speed In All Different Perspectives Screaming 'Helpppp'. All Done At Top Speed. Repeat Top Speed And On Grams – That Is, Recorded Records, Pre-recorded

WALLACE
Even as Seagoon is stricken with Spon, the British Medical Council are quick to seek a cure.

Grams: Duck Quacking

PETER (*Wolfit*)
Aaah, and so, gentlemen, I must conclude by drawing your attention to the fact that the use of leeches is not only useless but harmful.

OMNES
Paaah, ha, rubbish – man's unbalanced. He'll lose his stethoscope licence.

PETER (*confident idiot of middle age*)
Hur, hur. Gentlemen, I maintain that I have used leeches for years, and not one of them has ever been ill.

HARRY
Bravo, there's proof.

PETER
I might add that neither have I received any complaints from the patients' next of kin.

Grams: Old Men's Applause

FX: Door Bursts Open

NED
Stop stip stup stap stop. Gentlemen, grave news! A new malignant plague is upon us.

PETER
Oh, gooooood. Business is looking up.

NED
Who's business is looking up?

PETER
Bird-watchers. Ha he he . . .

NED
It's the plague, I tell you, the fearful and fearsome plague.

SPIKE
Splendid, we haven't had a good plague for years.

PETER
Yes, you get out of touch.

NED
Gentlemen, every patient that I examined this morning at a nominal fee of twenty guineas has the Spon Plague. Even I have it at a nominal fee of two and sixpence. The symptoms are bare knees – roll your trouser legs up.

Grams: Several Wooden Venetian Blinds Being Pulled Up Sharply With a Clatter

PETER
Oh, dearrrr. We got it.

NED
There's only one cure. Try and run away from your knees!

Grams: Great Protesting Quacking By Drakes and Ducks. Boots Running Into Distance

Orchestra: Dramatic Chords

WALLACE
The Spon Plague spread like wild-fire. Everywhere people were going down with it. Several people went *up* with it, and one gentleman was known to have gone sideways with it. The country was in a turmoil – as one Minister remarked –

PETER
They've never had it so good.

WALLACE
Meantime, in a new satellite town slum –

Grams: Rain Pouring Down Onto Floor, Musical Sound of Rain, Drops Plopping Into Small Pools of Water

CRUN
Oooh, dear . . . dearrrr dearrrr . . . oh dearrrr . . . Min? Modern Min?

MINNIE
What is it, cocky?

CRUN
Where have you put the roof?

MINNIE
I sent it to the menders, it was leaking, cocky.

CRUN
Oh, dearrrr. It's freezing cold in here, Min.

MINNIE
Well, sit nearer to Africa, it's warmer there.

CRUN
Oh yes! Nothing like an Africa to keep you warm, Min.

WALLACE
Yes, folks – do away with dirty coal – keep yourselves warm with Africa. Africa is now on sale to anyone who wants to make it a second India.

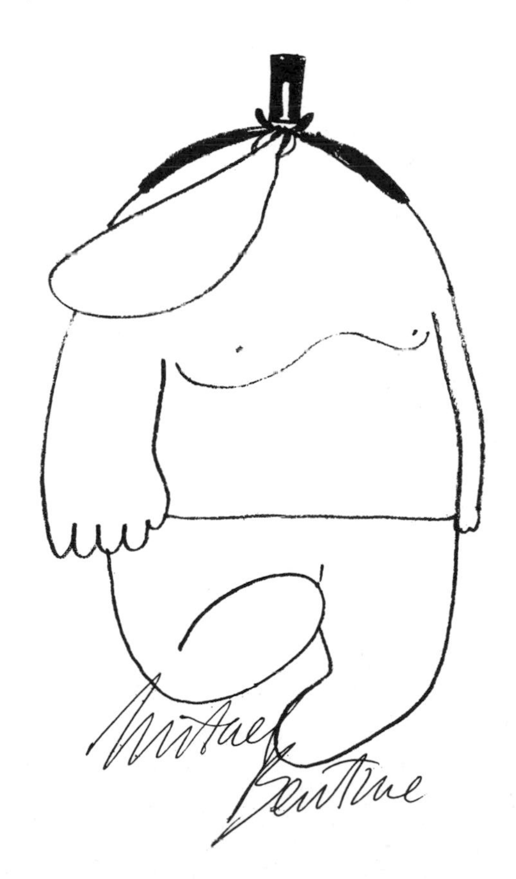

CRUN
Hear that, Min?

MINNIE
They knock Africa down and build flats there.

CRUN
I wish Disraeli was back.

MINNIE
He will be, Henery, he's just gone down to the shops.

FX: Knock On Door

MINNIE
Ah, that's him. Come in!

FX: Door Opens

MINNIE & CRUN
Morning, morning.

CRUN
Come in, Doctor Ned.

MINNIE
How's the Spon Plague?

CRUN
Oh, Doctor, is there no cure?

NED
None.

FX: Door Opens

THYNNE
News, Ned. I've found the cure – this bottle of pills. Ten shillings, please.

FX: Till

THYNNE
Ta, Ned, and a sailor's farewell.

Grams: Queen Mary's Hooter

NED
And so saying, he went through the door and disappeared into the night.

THYNNE
Did I? Well, I might have been told a bit sooner than this.

NED
And so saying, he went through . . .

THYNNE
Yes, they know . . .

NED
So saying, I read the instructions on the pills. Take three paces south, stretch our right arm, roll down trouser legs.

FX: Wooden Venetian Blinds Rolling Down

NED
Eureka! Huzza, folks, my bare knees have gone! Taxi!

Grams: Explosion

MATE
Yerst, mate?

NED
The Ministry of Health and Dirt, please.

MATE
Ta.

Grams: Bloodnok Theme. Bubbling Cauldron. Explosions

BLOODNOK
Gad, I can't send these to the laundry. There *must* be a cure for this. I can't go in the street, I –

Grams: Explosion

BLOODNOK
Ooooh, a taxi.

NED
Yes, it's the new type.

BLOODNOK
Come in.

NED
I am in.

BLOODNOK
Oh, he am in.

NED
Bloodnok, I've come here on business.

BLOODNOK
It's the quickest way. I always travel on business. Sit down.

FX: Duck Call

BLOODNOK
Eeehohhhhh . . . Every chair a whoopee cushion. Now, here's my brochure. And an interesting health picture of Sabrina.

NED
Thank you, and here is a picture of her clothes.

BLOODNOK
Good heavens, who's that man inside 'em?

ECCLES
It's me.

BLOODNOK
Get out, you fool. Now, Ned. Ohhh, oh dear, that's quite upset me.

NED
Bloodnok, here's a statue waiting to be unveiled.

FX: Heavy Tearing

BLOODNOK
Oooh, it's a statue of you saying –

Grams: Harry (Pre-Recorded) Saying 'I've Discovered A Cure For Spon Plague'

BLOODNOK
Thank you. And here is a wood carving of me saying –

Grams: Bubbling Cauldron. Explosion

BLOODNOK
Oooh, there *must* be a cure for it.

NED
Yes, and that cure is these anti-Spon pills.

BLOODNOK
Splendid. Now, sir, you'll find my static water tank in the attic.

NED
I'm not interested in your water tank.

BLOODNOK
So, that's your attitude. Well, sir, I'm not interested in *your* water tank.

NED
What? You're insulting the plumbing I love. Just for that, take that!

MAX (*very loud*)
Ploogieeeee!

BLOODNOK
It's Max Geldray! Run for it.

Grams: Thundering Feet Into The Distance With Small Explosions, and Screams By Bloodnok

Max & Orchestra: Music

WALLACE
Max Geldray is now appearing at the St James's Theatre. Mr Geldray will shortly be knocked down to make way for offices. I have great pleasure in announcing the chord of C.

Orchestra: Chord in C (Nice and Big)

Grams: Great Shovelling of Money. Coins Everywhere – Rolling Along The Ground

THYNNE
Hear that sound, folks? Money – M-O-N-E-Y, pronounced –

Grams: Grytpype-Thynne (Pre-Recorded), Slightly Faster, Saying 'Moneyyyyyy'

MORIARTY
Yes, Grytpype, the anti-Spon pills are selling like wild-fire. Ah hahahahahahah.

FX: Knock On Door. Door Opens

THYNNE
Yes?

WALLACE
Meantime, in a Government Laboratory.

THYNNE
Thank you.

FX: Door Closes

Grams: Fade In Bubbling Cauldron

MORIARTY
Listen, I can hear the best brains that low wages can buy.

BLUEBOTTLE
Don't take any notice of dem, Eccles. Now, my man, to our works. Remember, we're boy scientists working for our country. Picks up Union Jack, cleans boots.

ECCLES
Here, Bottle, I got a rise yesterday.

BLUEBOTTLE
How much?

ECCLES
Tree inches.

BLUEBOTTLE
Oh, what did you getted dat for, brainy?

ECCLES
I wrote a tune.

BLUEBOTTLE
Oh, play it, den.

ECCLES
OK.

Grams: Hammering of Nails in Wood

ECCLES
Hoi!

BLUEBOTTLE
Coo, I wish I was musical.

ECCLES
Come on, den, now all join in the chorus.

Grams: Great Mass of Hammering Nails In Wood At Different Tempos

WALLACE (*over*)
What a grand sight to see the studio audience hammering nails into each other.

FX: Spot Effect Carries On Hammering With The Above

BLUEBOTTLE
'Ray for tunes! Now to the anti-Spon experiment. Roll up your trousers for the injection.

FX: Wooden Blind Rolled Up

BLUEBOTTLE
Here, you're cured – you ain't got bare knees.

ECCLES
No, I always wear long underpants.

BLUEBOTTLE
Oh, den we got the answer to Spon.

Orchestra: Dramatic Chords

NED
Yes, folks, the Ministry of Health acted immediately. Within thirty years everyone had been immunized with long woollen underpants.

MORIARTY
Owwww, we're ruined. R-U-I-N-E-D, pronounced –

Grams: Moriarty (Pre-Recorded) Saying 'Ruineddddddd'

THYNNE (*furious*)
Foiled by long woollen things, but I'll get even, mark 'ee. Taxi!

Grams: Explosion

SPRIGGS
Where to, Jim, where to, Jimmmm?

THYNNE
Drive me up the wall.

SPRIGGS
Wo, wo wo wo wo wo wo wo.

THYNNE
Thank you. How much?

SPRIGGS
That's four and six, pronounced –

Grams: Spriggs (Pre-Recorded) Saying 'Tennnnn Bob'

THYNNE
Right, take it out of this.

FX: Pistol Shot

SPRIGGS
Thank you, Jim.

THYNNE
Moriarty, where's Neddie?

MORIARTY
In Scotland.

THYNNE
Right, let's go to him.

Grams: Whoosh. Bagpipes in Distance

NED
Hello, Grytpype, how nice to see you lads.

THYNNE
Bad news, Ned. Roll up your kilt.

FX: Whistle Up

MORIARTY
Oww owww.

THYNNE
Not too high, Ned . . . Gad, he's got it, Moriarty!

NED
Got what? What what?

THYNNE
You've got the Quodge.

NED
The Quodge? What's the symptoms?

THYNNE
It's bare knees covered with long underpants.

NED
I've got 'em, I've got the Quodge!

Grams: Harry (Pre-Recorded) Screaming 'Hellpppp!'. Running Boots

Orchestra: Dramatic Chords

PETER (*Scottish*)
The Quodge spread through Scotland like wild-fire. The hospitals were full of Quodge victims. It was a terrible sight ter see those knees covered with long underpants. So that the disease didna spread, a great wall was built by the English ter keep the Quodge north of the border. Contractor – Jim Hadrian.

Grams: Wind Howling On Moor. Distant Bagpipes. Horse Approaches

SENTRY
Halt – who gaes theere, the noo?

LALKAKA
Please do not shoot. We are two Indian gentlemen Western-style. We are here to investigate the Quodge on behalf of the Indian Government.

SENTRY
Advance and be recognized.

BANAJEE
I don't see the point, sir. You have never seen us before, therefore it is in the extreme of possibilities that you will recognize us.

LALKAKA
I must concur with Mr Banajee. I can recognize him and he in turn can recognize me.

BANAJEE
There is much truth in what you say, Mr Lalkaka.

LALKAKA
Indeed, man, yes. Every morning I am arising from my charpoy and looking in the mirror, I am seeing myself and I say 'Hello, there, there you are again, my fine fellow.'

SENTRY
You'll both get a bullet up yer back if you're no away.

LALKAKA
Please, European soldier, let's explain we are selling ties.

FX: Shots. Screams

Grams: Lalkaka & Banajee (Pre-Recorded) Screaming In Hindu. Running Feet Speeded Up, Like Wet Fish Being Slapped

THYNNE
Well done, sentry, it's patriotism like that that's made Egypt what it is today.

SENTRY
Oh, and what is it today?

MORIARTY
It's Thursday.

SENTRY
Oh, it's ma day off.

Grams: Whoosh

THYNNE
Right, open the gates, Moriarty, and let the stricken masses through.

FX: Great Bolt Slides Back Quickly

Grams: Great Yelling Masses, Bagpipes, All Playing At Speed

THYNNE
This way, Scottish people — don't panic — I have here on this stall a cure for the Quodge.

Orchestra: A Rararararararar Rarrrr.

FX: Till Ringing Up Over And Over Again

THYNNE
Thank you — ta — ta — one over there . . . (*Fades behind* —)

NED
Ha, ha, the swine didn't recognize me — I got a bottle — what's it say?

Grams: Peter (Pre-Recorded) Saying In Idiot Voice 'To Cure The Quodge, Swallow The Pills'

NED
Gad, a talking bottle . . . (*Gulps*)

Grams: Peter (Pre-Recorded) Saying In Idiot Voice 'Yes, Now Remove Long Underpants'

FX: Ripping

NED
Gad, cured! Not a trace of long underpants left — but wait — bare knees! I've got the Spon again!

THYNNE
I have the cure here.

FX: Till

NED
Swallow pill, pull on underpants — cured! Wait a minute — long underpants? The Quodge!

WALLACE
Dinner is served, gentlemen.

NED
Oh, down to the old canteen then. Goodnight, folks.

WALLACE
You can come out now, it's all over. Pronounced —

Grams: Wallace (Pre-Recorded) Saying 'Overrrrrrrr'

Orchestra: Old Comrades March

Tales of Men's Shirts

(Series 10)
Transmission: Thursday, 31 December 1959
Studio: The Camden Theatre, London

CAST

Harry Secombe
Lieutenant Neddie Seagoon

Peter Sellers
Major Dennis Bloodnok
Mate
Quarter-Master-General Henry Crun
Captain Grytpype-Thynne
Seaman Bluebottle
Von Arlone

Spike Milligan
Minnie Bannister
Eccles
Comte della Robbia Moriarty

With The Ray Ellington Quartet, Max Geldray,
and the Orchestra conducted by Wally Stott.
Script by Spike Milligan.
Announcer Wallace Greenslade.
Producer Charles Chilton.

WALLACE
This is the BBC. After the news there will be a talk on Early Christian Plastic Knees, and the first broadcast of a piece of knotted string. If you would like a piece of knotted string, send three rust-proof shillings to 'Honest' Wal Greenslade of Weybridge. Ta.

NED
Hello folks, hello folks, and in that order!

WALLACE
Ta. That voice comes from inside a short fat round blob, namely Neddie of Wales.

NED
My first impression will be of Peter Sellers.

PETER
Hello folks.

Grams: Sudden Burst of Cheering

NED
Stop! My next impression will be of Spike Milligan saying 'Thynne'.

SPIKE
Thynneeeeeeeeeeeeeeeeeeee!

Orchestra & Omnes: Thynneeeeeeeeeeeeeeeeeeee!

Orchestra: Thynneeeeeeeeeeeeeeeeeeee!

NED
That's thin enough! Remember, folks, saying 'Thynneeeee' cures you of monkeys on the knees.

PETER
Yes, if you've got monkeys on the knees, just say –

SPIKE
Thynneeeeeeeeeeeeeeeeeeee!

PETER
And they are only three and six a box.

SPIKE
Yes, I swear by them. One morning I woke up and there they were – monkeys on the knees!

Grams: At The Word 'Monkeys' Add Sound Of Monkeys In a Temper

SPIKE
Then I said the cure word – Thynneeeeeeeeeeeeee!

Grams: Speed Up and Fade Record of the Monkeys At High Speed

WALLACE
Ta. The monkeys were played by professional apes.

NED
That was Wallace Greenslade saying words.

WALLACE
Mr Seagoon, stand by to take part in an adventure story entitled –

Orchestra: Timpani Roll Soft – Held Under Speech

PETER
'Tales of Men's Shirts' – a story of down under.

Orchestra: Concluding Chords

Grams: Morse Code Comes Out of the Music

WALLACE
1938 – but from the continent come ominous rumblings.

Grams: Rumbling and Bubbling Cauldron.

BLOODNOK
Oh, this Spanish food! Waiter! One brandy – and pronto.

SPIKE (*Jim*)
One brandy and pronto coming up!

WALLACE
Those were the last words said at peace. At that moment Germany declared war in all directions.

SPIKE
Bang!

BLOODNOK
Bang? War!!! I must write me memoirs.

FX: Typewriter

BLOODNOK
The day war broke, I said to Allenbrooke, 'You fool . . .'

NED
England was mobilized.

PETER
Recruits were rushing to the recruiting depots at the rate of one a year.

WALLACE
We join the story in 1942, a critical year for Britain, with British Generals slaving away at their autobiographies.

Grams: Dozens of Typewriters

PETER (*American*)
While across the Channel, the German High Command were welding a master plan.

Grams: Typewriters

HARRY
Achtung, gentlemen! Be seated. We must have a halt on our war memoirs and go to war. Our scientists have just invented a liquid that will win der war. This chemical, when applied to the tail of a military soldier shirt, is tasteless, colourless and odourless.

SPIKE
What good is that on the tail of a shirt, hein?

HARRY
The moment the wearer sits down, the heat from his body causes the chemical to explode. This way, the soldier will be neutralized.

SPIKE
It will be worse than that.

PETER
Is einer wonderschön Gerhimmel!

HARRY
Speak English, you swine, there are no sub-titles in this scene. Now zen, this is my plan of attack.

SPIKE
It looks like a nail.

HARRY
No, it's a tack. Ho ho ho ho – who said we Germans haven't a sense of humour?

SPIKE
Just about everybody.

HARRY
Oberlieutenant Schatz! You will take ten men, each one carrying a spray-gun full of the exploding shirt-tail fluid. You will be dropped near Leicester and there you will gain entrance to the Great British Military Shirt Factory. The rest is up to you. We shall call the operation 'Burnbaum'.

Orchestra: German Chords

WALLACE
The effect of this deadly plan was soon felt. The first discovery was made at Whitehall, where they were working at their memoirs.

Grams: Typewriters

BLOODNOK
Halt! Now gentlemen – be seated.

Grams: Series of Shirt-Tail Explosions and Shouts of Rage

BLOODNOK
Ohhhhhh – quick, nurse, the screens!

WALLACE
Portions of the charred shirt-tails were soon at a Military Forensic Laboratory, where they were forensicked.

NED
Mmmm, yes, there's been severe combustion all right. Hard to say what type – what do you think, sir?

MATE
Ooo, I don' know, mate, I'm only the kleener around 'ere.

NED
Oh, I'm sorry, I thought you were one of us.

MATE
No, no – I'm one of them, mate.

NED
You don't look like one of them. I mean, why are you dressed like an admiral?

MATE
Well, I don't like people ter think I'm just a kleener. I mean, I went to a good school, mate – Eton.

NED
How long were you there?

MATE
Oh, about five minutes. I was deliverin' the groceries.

NED
You were a greengrocer?

MATE
Not quite green, more of a dirty yellow colour – ha ha ha . . .

NED
Very good, now just step out of this thirteenth-storey window.

MATE
No thanks, I'm trying to give 'em up.

NED
I wish I could   hup!

MATE (*dramatic*)
So sayin', he stepped aht –

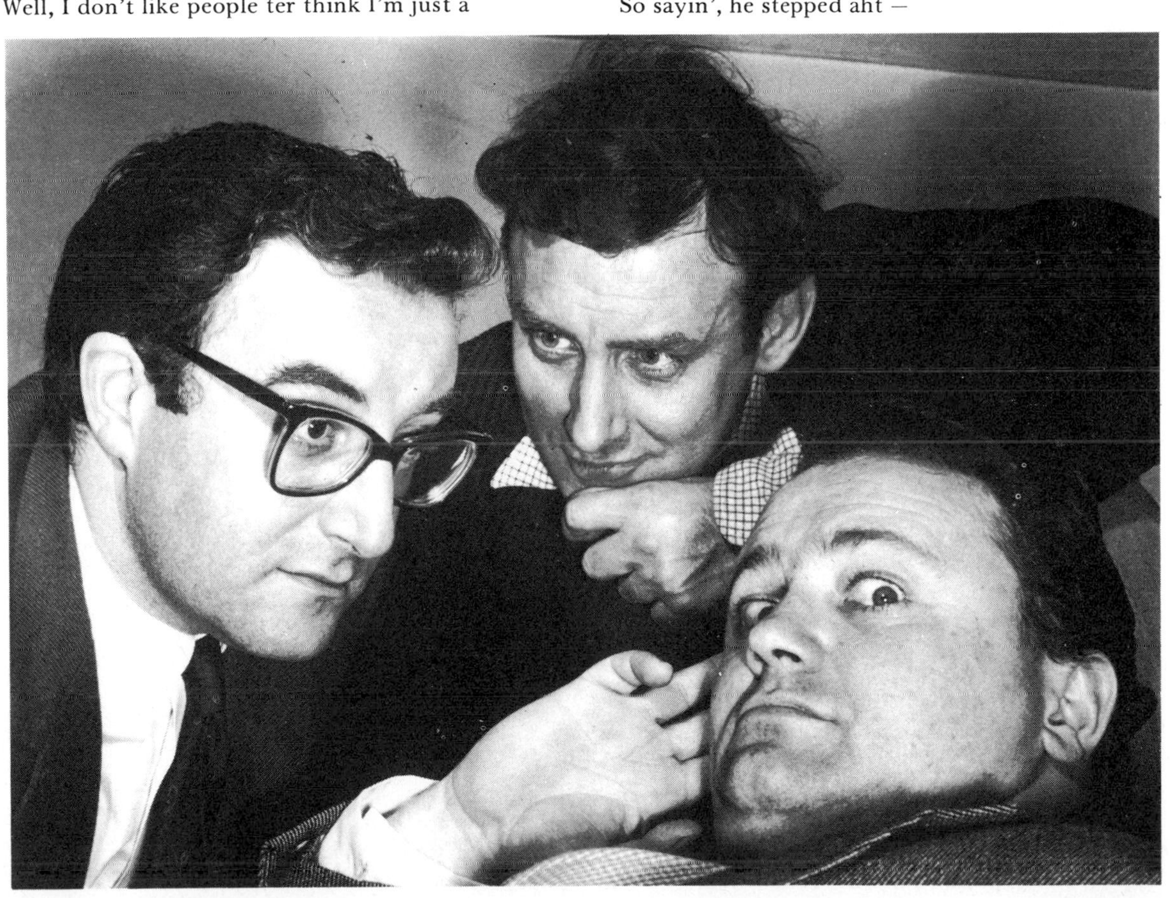

Grams: Long Fading Screammmmmmmmmm (Very Long Indeed)

NED
Yes, I always travel by window, folks, it's the quickest way down. I was on my way to the Quarter-Master-General. Nick Nock Nokkity Nok.

CRUN
Come in, Pnick Pnock Pnokkity Pnok.

NED
It's me – Lieutenant Seagoon – from the body of the same name.

CRUN
Oh, Ned. Here, let me take your window – eh – did you hear they're sending up a rocket to photograph the other side of you?

NED
All lies, all lies! I'm losing weight – I've dropped three stone.

FX: Lump of Iron Goes Clang on the Ground

NED
There's one now.

MINNIE
Hello, sailor.

NED
What's this, then?

MINNIE
My name is Bannister.

NED
Didn't I see you on the stairs?

MINNIE
Don't bother me . . .

FX: Typewriter

MINNIE
'I was Churchill's Wet Nurse', Chapter One. I was standing in Piccadilly when . . .

NED
Now, Mr. Crun, I want to borrow a stock military shirt for an experiment. But first, Geldray and his famed Dutch Conk!

MAX
These are my wartime Conk memoirs. Ploogie!

Max & Orchestra: Music

WALLACE
'Tales of Men's Shirts', Part Two.

Orchestra: Dramatic Descending Chords with Distant Bugle and Drum

Grams: Crowd of Men Chatting and Typewriters

PETER (*loud and soft voice*)
Eyes front, ears to the side! Stop these memoirs! Orderly Officer. . .

Grams: Slur Record of Chatting Down

PETER
All correct and present, sir. Thynneee!

NED
Thank you, and *Thynneee.* Right, at ease, men.

Grams: Immediate Snoring – Fade Under

NED
Gentlemen, all you officers have been selected because of your high standard of intelligence.

ECCLES
You sure of dat?

NED
Someone has blundered. Private Eccles, I've got bad news.

ECCLES
Private? I'm a Captain.

NED
That's the bad news. Now, just stand in this shallow grave and wait for the next death. Gentlemen, there has been an outbreak of exploding shirt-tails in the British Army. We suspect sabotage.

SPIKE (*gabbles a rubbishy question*)

NED
Not when the train is standing in the station.

SPIKE
Blast!

NED
Now, gentlemen, this is a matter of life and death. I want a volunteer to wear this shirt and make notes on the way it behaves. In fact, try everything to make that shirt-tail explode. Who will volunteer?

Omnes: Pause – Light, Nervous Singing Starts – Gets Louder and Louder

Orchestra: All Gradually Join In the Singing

The Goons with model Barbara Goalen in 1958

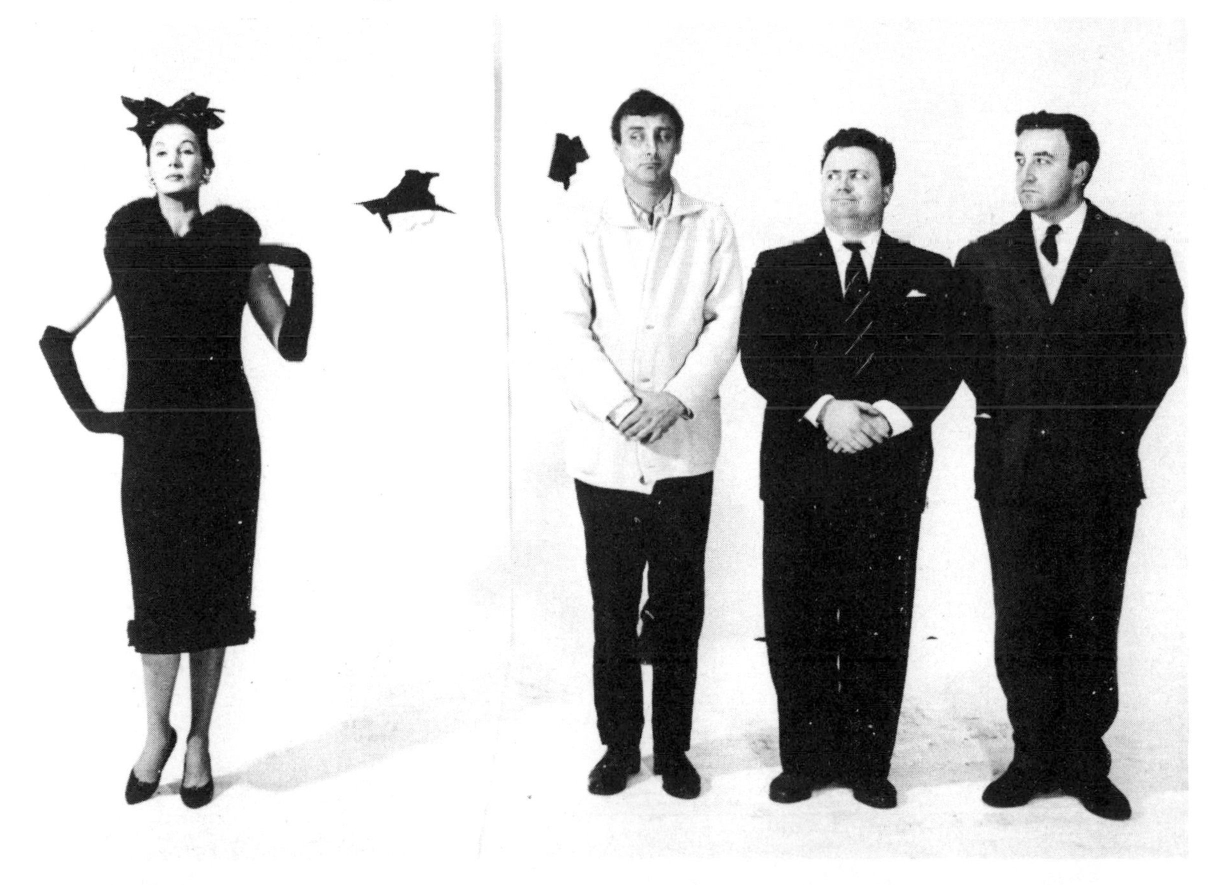

NED
Stop this! I appreciate your love of singing and cowardice – if you won't volunteer, we must draw lots. Eccles? Write your name on a piece of paper and put it in this hat.

ECCLES
Dere.

NED
Now draw it out and read it.

ECCLES
Mrs Phyllis Quott.

NED
You imposter, you're not Mrs Quott.

ECCLES
Wait, I know the ideal volunteer for you – he's had more experience with shirt-tails than anybody – his name is –

Orchestra: Bloodnok Theme

FX: Typewriter

BLOODNOK
So I said to Winnie, 'Allenbrooke and Montgomery are ideal lads –'

Grams: The Shirt-Tail Explosion

BLOODNOK
Oh oh – Abdul! Quick, a new shirt – it's happened again.

NED
Nickity Knock Knock oh nock!

BLOODNOK
Nickity Knock Knock oh nock? That's my private number. Come in within.

NED
Thank you. Major Bloodnok?

BLOODNOK
I have been called worse. Yes? Now what can I do for you? Better still, *get out*!!!!!!!!!

NED
Major, I'm here to offer you money.

BLOODNOK
Ohhhh, come in Ned, warm yourself by this woman. She's just coming to the boil.

Grams: Kettle With Steam Whistle

BLOODNOK
There she goes!!!

NED
I've been told that you have more experience with exploding shirt-tails than any man alive.

BLOODNOK
True. I feel no pain. But what of the rewards?

NED
Several plastic OBEs and a drip-dry statue of Diana Dors and a ticket to Hampstead Fairground.

BLOODNOK
Ohhhh, none but the brave deserve the fair.
I accept!

NED
Come, Bloodnok, on with this military test shirt.

BLOODNOK
Let's drink to the success of the venture – here's mud in yer eye.

NED (*puzzled*)
So saying, he threw a plate of mud at me.

Orchestra: Dramatic Chords

WALLACE
Neddy's next move was to actually get into Germany and try to find out the enemy's secret.

NED
At dawn, a ship hove to at Portsmouth Ho.

Grams: Seagulls. Bosun's Whistle. Ship Making Up Steam

FX: Typewriter

MORIARTY
'How I Saved De Gaulle And Told Mark-Clarke Where To Get Off . . .' (*Sings*) A life on the ocean waveee, is the key to a watery grave.

THYNNE
Happy, Moriarty?

MORIARTY
Aye aye, Captain.

NED
Ahoy there!

THYNNE
Ahoy, Ned! Come aboard.

Grams: Splash

THYNNE
You must wait for the gangplank – ups-a-daisy.

Grams: Man Pulled Out of Water

NED
Jove, that water was taller than me!

THYNNE
It's older, that's why. Welcome to the Good Ship Lollipop.

NED
My name is Lieutenant Seagoon.

THYNNE
A better name for a twit I've yet to hear. Ned, this man in the red football jersey and one white sock is an old French sailor.

MORIARTY
Aye, mate, I've got the sea in my blood.

NED (*giggles*)
And you can see where it gets in.

MORIARTY
Mind how you speak to me. Do you know who I am?

NED
Can't you remember?

MORIARTY
I am Comte della Robbia Moriarty, the Duke of Orange, an old naval family.

NED
So, folks, he comes from a long line of naval oranges – ha ha ha ha. Laugh and the world laughs with you, they say.

THYNNE
You've proved them wrong, haven't you?

SPIKE (*Jim*)
We're ready to sail, Jim, ready to saillllllllll.

THYNNE
Thank you, Jimmmmmm! Cast off fore and aft and ift.

Omnes: Sea Shouts

Grams: Ship's Telegraph

Orchestra: Dramatic Seascape Music

WALLACE
A heavy sea mist descended, demanding constant vigilance by seamen in the chart-room.

BLUEBOTTLE
Aft by fore aft . . . Six bells and all's well on the dog. (*Sings*)

NED
Everything all right, Seaman Bottle?

BLUEBOTTLE
Everything is Bristol fashion and shipn-shanke.

NED
Aye aye.

BLUEBOTTLE
Aye aye to *you*, sir. De de de (*sings*) de de de de de.

NED
What's that rough sailor song you sing, Seaman?

BLUEBOTTLE
I'm singing this map . . . (*Ad libs tune*) All those brown parts are the land, and the blue bits with the little lines on are the seasssssssss, all the green is where the forest is, Sherwood Forest nine miles long . . .

NED (*singing with Bottle*)
Ahh lad, they don't write maps like that any more. I say, this fog is getting thick.

Grams: Distant Fog Horn. Bloodnok's 'Ohhhhhh'

NED
What's that?

BLUEBOTTLE
Sounds like Major Bloodnok.

NED
No, it can't be. He's never had it that bad . . . Is Eccles in the crow's nest?

BLUEBOTTLE
Yes . . .

NED
Eccles?

ECCLES
Yer.

NED
Can you see ahead?

ECCLES
Yer, a big bald one.

NED
Is it one of ours?

ECCLES
Ray Ellington on the cardboard bow!

RAY
Man! I don't know how they get away with it.

The Ray Ellington Quartet: Music

WALLACE
That was Mr Ray Ellington, who now uses the blue whitener. Part Three of 'Tales of Men's Shirts'. Thynneeeee!

Orchestra: Dramatic Return-to-Story Chords

NED
At dawn we came to off the coast of Germany. We prepared to swim ashore by electric plunging drawers.

THYNNE
No you don't! Hands up, little Ned of Wales.

NED
What's the meaning of this?

THYNNE
This means you're a prisoner of the German Navy.

NED
So that's what *this* means. I've often wondered. You traitor, Thynne.

THYNNE
My name is Horne.

NED
Traitor Horne!

Orchestra: Ta Raa Cymbal

NED
They don't come any older.

THYNNE
Moriarty, clap this lot in irons.

FX: Typewriters

THYNNE
Chapter Two: 'How I Captured a British Idiot in Drawers'.

MORIARTY
Come on, you – spotty Herbert.

BLUEBOTTLE
Take your hands of me! Do you think you take Bluebottle alive? Fixes Moriarty with hypnotic gaze – toot toot toot . . .

Grams: Old Fashioned Silent Movie Piano – Tension Music

BLUEBOTTLE
My man, I was trained in Judo by the Great Bert. Using the body as a counter-pivot to displace the opponent, I use the Great Bert's method of throwing the opponent to his death. Be warned, Moriarty, one false move and you die by Bert's method.

MORIARTY
Take that!

FX: Thwack on Bottle's Head

BLUEBOTTLE
Owwwww! (*Cries*) Wait till I see that twit Bert . . .

ECCLES
You hit my friend Bottle again and see what happens.

FX: Terrific Slapstick

BLUEBOTTLE
Owwwwwww!

ECCLES
See? Dat's what happens!

Orchestra: Dramatic Descending Chords

FX: Typewriter

WALLACE
'The Greenslade War Memoirs', Chapter One. I said to Allenbrooke, 'How dare you . . .'

Grams: Behind Dialogue: Silent Film Piano – Sad

WALLACE
The whole plot has misfired. Lieutenant Seagoon has somehow been betrayed. The destroyer transferred them to a U-boat that took them to the POW camp at Rhinegold Castle.

SPIKE
The prison was full of British Officers who had sworn to die rather than be captured.

NED
It was winter when we arrived and the snow lay heavy on the slopes of Brigitte Bardot.

VON ARLONE
Nowzen, Englanders, my name is von Arlone.

ECCLES (*sings*)
Von Aloneeeeee ter be –

FX: Slapstick

ECCLES
Owwww, you'll pay fer dat.

FX: Half A Crown Thrown Down Onto the Pavement

ECCLES
Ta. Want another go?

NED
Shut up, Eccles. Now then, von Arlone, what do you intend to do with us?

VON ARLONE
You will be incarcerated.

NED
Ahemmm. I hope I heard right.

VON ARLONE
Perhaps if you were to tell us what your mission is, we could . . .

NED
Never – I won't tell you!

VON ARLONE
Do you know what happens to British spies?

NED
No.

VON ARLONE
So, you won't even tell us *that*? Throw them in Stalag Ten – Eleven – and Twelve! Gerschmeltentwitz!

Orchestra: Dramatic Chords

Grams: Iron Door Slams. Heavy Key in Lock. Pair of Gaolers' Footsteps Walk Away

BLUEBOTTLE
I don't like this game. I don't like all these hairy Germans, they hitted me. Hitttt . . . Hitttt . . . Hitteeeeeeee, they went.

NED
Don't worry men. I have a plon of a plan. When the German guard comes in with our dinner, let him have it!

BLUEBOTTLE
Den what are we going to eat?

NED
I mean, let him have this iron bar on his nut, then we'll change uniforms and pretend to be Huns. Trouble is, I can't speak the language. Eccles, how's your German?

ECCLES
He's fine, how's yours?

MATE (*approaching, singing*)
Deutschland, Deuescher land uber the alles, mate.

NED
Listen – a German speaking fluent Cockney.

FX: Iron Gate Opening

MATE
Here's yer breakfast, mates.

FX: Great Heavy Rock Thuds on The Floor

MATE
Boiled egg, I'll be bound, ha ha –

FX: Iron Bar Across His Nut

MATE
Oh, I been sponned – from the film of the same nameeeeee. Ohhhhhh.

FX: Feeble Typewriter

MATE (*very feeble*)
Chapter One: 'How I was Sponned in Action'. I said to Alanbrooke, 'You twit . . .'

NED
Wait – this isn't a German, this is Sewerman Sam! What are you doing dressed as a German General?

MATE
I told yer, I don't like people to know I does the sewers.

NED
You come with us. You may come in useful – you can say odd lines.

MATE
Odddd Linessssss! Odd Liness! Yer, I can.

Orchestra: Dramatic Chords

WALLACE
Ned and his party made their way to the great German Chemical Works at Schattz. By using the short-wave cardboard secret horse-hair and mattress telephone, they were able to contact London by speech.

FX: Typewriter on Distort

BLOODNOK (*distorted*)
Hello, hello – Lieutenant Seagoon, about artillery –

NED
What about it?

BLOODNOK
One '1' or two?

NED
Two '1'.

BLOODNOK
To 'ell with you, too.

NED
We've escaped from the German nick.

BLOODNOK
German Nick? That swine, he and Belgian Tom!

Now listen, we've discovered the name of the chemical that explodes our shirt-tails. It's called Gerschattzer.

NED
Gerschattzer? How do you spell it?

BLOODNOK
I – T

NED (*over writing FX*)
I – T, pronounced Gerschattzer . . . Thanks. Now, will you do us a favour?

BLOODNOK
What's her name?

NED
Women – women – is that all you think of?

BLOODNOK (*meditatively*)
By Jove, I do believe it is. Naughty Dennis.

NED
Listen, I remember in the First World War that an English Officer hid in a cupboard from the Germans. So could you have three cupboards dropped to us?

BLOODNOK
At once.

Grams: Crash Crash Crash

NED
Thank you. Now men, the moment you see any Germans approaching, swallow your uniforms, get inside the cupboards, and do an impression of a suit – the shabbier the better.

BLUEBOTTLE
Can I be a pin-stripe, Captain?

NED
No, I want the pin-stripe – I'm senior.

ECCLES
I'll be a morning suit so I can have the afternoon off.

BLOODNOK
I'll be a dinner jacket – I'm hungry.

NED
Bloodnok! Come out of that cupboard!

BLOODNOK
Has her husband gone, then?

NED
This is not the time to think of women.

BLOODNOK
Well, let me know when it is and I'll be off again. OOOOOOh.

Grams: Chickens Clucking

NED (*dry*)
Look – a patrol of Germans disguised as chickens.

BLOODNOK
Nonsense – they're disguised as pigeons.

NED
So that's why we've all been spotted.

BLOODNOK
Shh! Look, they're digging in behind that tree. I *hope* they're digging in behind that tree.

NED
Shhh . . . Keep quiet. They know we're here. I wonder why they're holding their fire.

ECCLES
Perhaps they haven't got a fireplace.

FX: Slapstick

SPIKE
Listen, Englanders – ve know you are dere.

NED
Gad, it's Spike Milligan with a bad German accent.

SPIKE
Listen, we make bargain – we let you all go free if you hand over Major Bloodnok.

BLOODNOK
Never! You hear? We'd rather die than hand him over.

NED
You speak for yourself.

BLOODNOK
I am. I'll make a bargain with you! Take all these lads and I'll let Major Bloodnok go free. What do you say?

SPIKE
Dis is our answer.

FX: Great Outbreak of Firing

BLOODNOK
Speak English, you swine!

Grams: American Bugle Call and Approach of Cavalry. Shooting

NED
Look – the American Fifth Cavalry! Saved!

Orchestra: Ta Raa

WALLACE
That was ending Number One. And now here is happy ending Number Two.

Orchestra: Alto and Rhythm Play 'Laura'

FX: Door Opens

NED
Cynthia? Cynthia darling, it's me – Tom.

PETER
Tom darling! You're back!

NED
Yes. I've been a fool about you.

PETER
Don't say that, darling.

NED
This parcel – it's – it's for you.

PETER
Ohh – what is it?

FX: Unwrapping

NED
Darling, this thing is bigger than both of us.

PETER
Oh, Tom, it's – it's an elephant!

NED
Yes – I'm not waiting any longer, we're getting married tonight.

WALLACE
And so, that night, Neddie Seagoon married an elephant. Goodnight.

Orchestra: Old Comrades March

Robin's Post

(Series 6)
Transmission: Tuesday, 6 December 1955
Studio: The Camden Theatre, London

CAST

Peter Sellers

Patsy Hagen
Major Dennis Bloodnok
Grytpype-Thynne
Henry Crun
Bluebottle

Spike Milligan

Fred Fumanchu
Throat
Moriarty
Minnie Bannister
Eccles

Harry Secombe
Chief Commissioner Neddie Seagoon

With The Ray Ellington Quartet, Max Geldray,
and the Orchestra conducted by Wally Stott.
Script by Spike Milligan.
Announcer Wallace Greenslade.
Producer Peter Eton.

WALLACE
This is the BBC. It feareth not, and holdeth forth not, but it keepeth friends with alleth.

NED
And a ripe twit thou soundest. What's all this 'thim them thou' chat?

WALLACE
Chat? Well, we felt that in strict contrast with the coming brisk clinical commercial radio, we might introduce an olde worlde atmosphere.

NED
A good answer, now read the statues on this Monogrammed Water Buffaloo.

WALLACE
In the absence of entertainment we present –

Orchestra: Tatty Gong

PETER
The Great Brown, all the way from mysterious Upper Dicker. No question is too difficult.

JIM
First question?

HARRY (*Twitt*)
My name is Gladys Clutt.

JIM
There is no cure. Next!

HARRY (*Twitt*)
No, my name is Gladys Clutt spelt with a Masculine G as in Gee Whizz.

PETER
I'm his friend.

JIM
Just stand in this open crocodile and wait for the first spring swallow.

NED
Who won the Battle of Waterloo?

JIM
Tom Kretch.

NED
Wrong! It was Lord Wellington.

JIM
It's only your word against mine, Jim.

Orchestra: Taa Raaaaaaa Ching (On Real Old Cymbal)

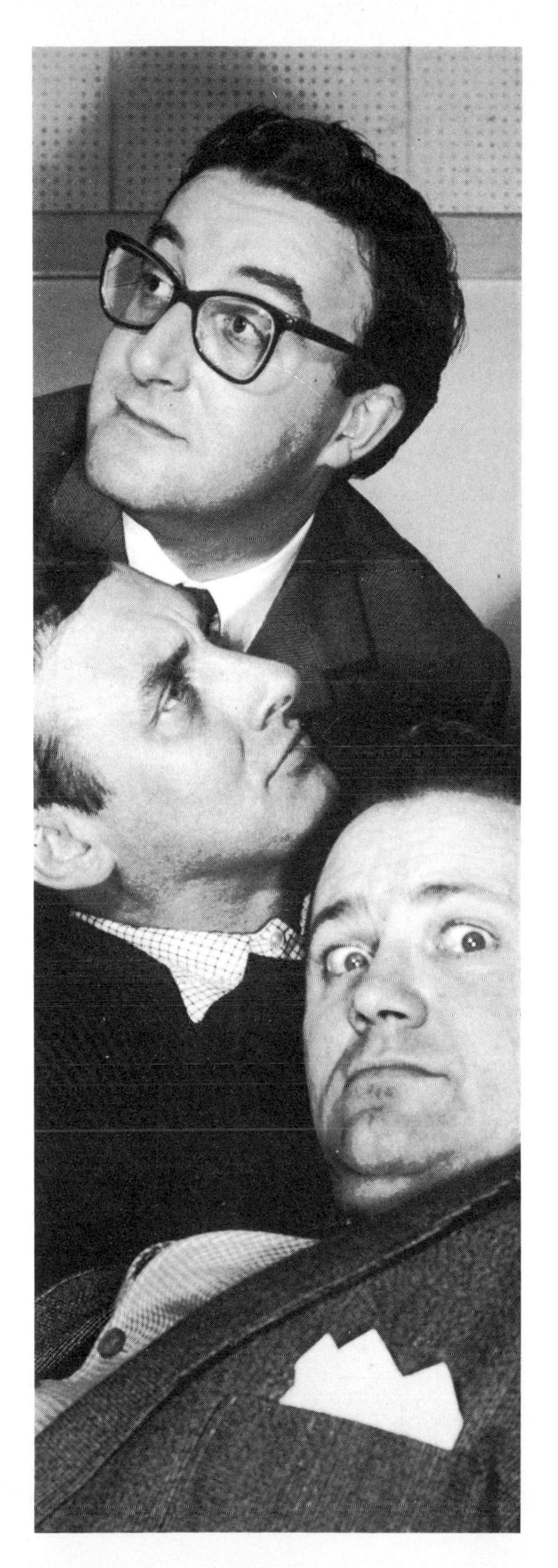

PETER (*gushing BBC twit announcer*)
And this week's 'Workers Playtime' came from a cake-bottling factory in Burton Wood. Now, here is the foreman's name –

NED
Tom Hopkin.

Grams: Roars of Laughter. Goats and Cows

WALLACE
That was the sound of the human race – resignation forms are now available. Now, to certain things –

PETER (*Swede*)
Aye to that, sirr.

WALLACE
The part of the Cornish idiot was played at short notice by a very well-known Cornish idiot player.

PETER
Harr . . . narnnnnnnnnnn.

WALLACE
Ta. We present a tragedy – the story of Lord Seagoon, playboy of the Western Approaches, great lover, man of action, athlete, slob – and great wit.

NED
Who's a great twit?

Orchestra: Dramatic Chords

Grams: Old Time Orchestra Playing The Lancers In The Distance. Murmur Of The Dancers

SPIKE
Jove, you look lovely tonight, Daphne.

PETER
Oh, you're just saying that.

SPIKE
Let's go into the garden.

NED
Hear that maddening sound of gaiety, music and acting? Huh huh huh . . . It took place in Robin's Post, my ancestral home at Hailsham, Sussex, S.W.3. Now, it's all gone. G-o-n-e pronounced –

Grams: Spike (Pre-Recorded) saying very fast 'Goneeeeeeeeee'

NED
I was rich, as you will now hear.

Grams: Ned (Pre-Recorded) saying slightly faster than normal 'I was rich'

NED
This is me now speaking, a ruined, broken, crumbling man, going to pieces.

FX: Length of the Tubular Bell From the Tubular Bells. Let Drop On The Floor

NED
There goes another bit.

PETER
After her, men.

NED
Her? Yes, it was a woman who brought me this low – that and short legs.

Grams: Quack of Duck

NED
Duck's disease, the curse of the Seagoons. Anyhow, we met years ago. Her name was Penelope, mine was Ned. Why, I can hear her now.

PETER (*old dear*)
Hello, Ned dear.

NED
There she is!!!!!! But let's go back to when it alllllll started. It was 1901 and I was holding a masked ball.

Grams: Surge Up The Dancers And The Music. Then Down

Omnes: Odd Lines of Chatter. 'Gad, She's Got A Trim Ankle', etc.

THYNNE (*approaches laughing*)
Ha ha ha, tell me Lord Seagoon, why are you holding that masked ball?

NED
This is no ordinary ball.

THYNNE
Don't frighten me, Ned.

NED
This man was the powerful Lord Thynne, power behind the throne, owner of *The Times*, Peer of the Realm and relief pianist at the Hackney Empire.

MORIARTY
Tell me, Neddie, what is that ball made from?

NED
Oh, silly old gold.

Grams: Moriarty (Pre-Recorded): Series Of Screams And Yells About Gold. Take Three Overlapping Tracks.

FX: Slapstick Fast Twice

THYNNE
Steady, Moriarty, it's only gold. Come, lets weigh it on this set of scales I happen to have handy . . . there.

Grams: Squeak of Scales

THYNNE
Fourteen carrots, three turnips and a mango – gad, it's worth its weight in greens.

NED
But what does it mean to me, Lord Thynne, me, a man of means?

ECCLES
Hello Neddie, Hello Neddie. Ho, phew, I've danced every dance since it started, Lancers, eightsome reels, tango, waltz.

NED
Who was the lucky girl?

ECCLES
I didn't bother about them, I did it on my own. I'm not the idiot you think I am.

THYNNE
Oh, which idiot are you then?

ECCLES
Ummmmmm, what I mean is, I'm a great thinker.

THYNNE
For instance?

ECCLES
For instance, I think . . . er . . . I think . . . I think I'll go home.

THYNNE
You thought of that all by yourself?

ECCLES
Well, if you put it like that – yes.

THYNNE
Mmmmm – time for Conks Geldray.

FX: Slapstick

Max & Orchestra: Music

MAX
That was the music of Conks Geldray, folks. Conks lets in the air.

WALLACE
Mr. Geldray wishes it known that the Conks Anonymous Club is now open for membership. Part Two of our Tragedy.

Grams: Old Time Music As Before. Music Stops – Polite Applause. Laughter of Dancers Leaving The Floor

NED
Between dances we sat on the balcony smoking port and drinking sherry.

THYNNE (*aside*)
Moriarty – stand by the light switch. Now, Ned, let's have a look at the golden ball.

Grams: Crackling of Electricity. Dancers Reaction

NED
Don't panic, folks. It's only the gas mantles fused – carry on dancing.

PETER (*Geraldo*)
What do you mean, man? The boys can't see to play in the dark.

NED
Come now, you can busk.

PETER
Only from music. In the dark we're strictly a load of schmose.

NED
Nonsense. Hand me an instrument, I'll play. Waltz, please.

Orchestra: Drums: Play Waltz Tempo

NED
And so the magic of my waltz rhythm rang through the hall (*Sings*) Fertang, fertang, fertang tang tang – but in the rosy light of dawn, I discovered myself sitting in the middle of a field in full evening dress playing the drums. I took immediate action – I stopped playing –

Grams: Ned (Pre-Recorded) Saying Normally 'Next Dance Pleaseeeeeeee'

NED
– I said.

MATE (*to self*)
Hello, we got a right twit 'ere.

NED
Ah, good morning, Constabule.

MATE
Hello, sonny, lost the band?

NED
No, someone has stolen Robin's Post, my ancestral home.

MATE (*slowly*)
'Ere, you haven't escaped from anywhere, have you?

NED
What do you mean?

MATE
You know – one of them. (*Puts finger in mouth – wobbles*) Wo wo wo wo.

NED
I say, how do you do that?

MATE
Wo wo wo wo.

NED
Here, let me try . . . Wo wo wo wo . . . ha ha ha ha . . . Let's do it together.

NED & MATE
Wo wo wo wo.

NED
I say this *is* fun.

MATE
And it's tax-free, mate. Now, come along, off to the station.

Grams: Ned (Pre-Recorded) Protesting 'No no no wo wo (Speed Up Slowly) I'm not wo wo wow – let me go'

MATE (*Over Grams & FX*)
Come on, a few powders and you'll be all right on it.

Orchestra: Soft Sad Long Dull Chord. Two Bar Hot Break On Trombone

WALLACE
Very puzzling. Part Two

FX: Rattling Iron Door

NED
Let me out of this place! Take this jacket off. (*Interrupts behind Wallace*)

WALLACE
Lord Seagoon had been incarcerated in a gentlemen's rest home in Sussex on a charge of going 'Wo wo wo wo wo', illusions of grandeur, and duck's disease. Wow wo wo wo wo – I say, it's not difficult – wo wo wo wo wo.

MATE
In you go, too.

Grams: Iron Door Slams

WALLACE
You can't lock me away, I'm from the BBC – wo wo wo wo wo wo.

MATE
Oh, you're just the right type, mate. Wo wo wo wo 'em, mate.

NED
It's no good, Wal. We'll plot to get out of here – I'll bake a cake, put a file in it and post it to myself –

JIM
Parcel for you!

NED
It's arrived!

FX: Rapid Ripping Open

NED
And here's the file. Now, while I claw a hole in the wall with my bare hands, you cover up the sound by filing through your teeth.

FX: Filing

BLOODNOK
I say, are you filing your teeth?

WALLACE
Yes.

BLOODNOK
Well put 'em under 'T'.

NED
Bloodnok! How did you get in here?

BLOODNOK
I have the OBE and a parcel of steamed squids.

NED
Shut up man – help me dig a tunnel.

Grams: Digging Up Rocks By Hand

BLOODNOK
Ohhhhhhhhhh . . . Ohhhhhhhh –

NED
You've *got* to get rid of these rocks –

BLOODNOK
I'm eating them as fast as I can!

NED & BLOODNOK (*grunting*)

Grams: Rocks being Piled

WALLACE
What are you doing, Mr. Seagoon?

NED
Twit! I'm trying to tunnel out.

BLOODNOK
Now, Ned of Wales, Bloodnock of Anywhere will get you out of this home provided you sign the contract on this boiled egg.

NED (*dry*)
Is this contract binding?

BLOODNOK
A real eye waterer. Now, let's have your deposit – this set of drums will do – gad, they look in fine military condition. I'll do a parrididdle on 'em.

NED
Don't you dare!!

Orchestra: Drums Play A Military Beat. Side Drum And Undampened Bass Drum

BLOODNOK (*over orchestra sings his favourite military melody. All fade into distance*)

NED
He's escaped by military drums. Thank heavens – he's gone.

BLOODNOK
And thank heavens – he's back again. 'The Return of Bloodnok', Part Three. (*Acts*) Hello, Neddie of Wales. Look, we've all been imprisoned here for wo wo wo and unlawfully detained as retired stud horses.

NED
Yes, why should we spend the rest of our time here?

BLOODNOK
True. I mean, I can still pull a cart and whistle the Queen (*Whistles tunelessly*)

NED
Look, this is *my* plan.

Grams: Series of Electronic Sounds

BLOODNOK
Oh. It sounds infalliable, when do we start?

NED
Now. First we must contact a solicitor. Contact.

CRUN
Contact.

Grams: Propeller-Engined Plane Roars Into Life Then Slurs To A Stop

CRUN
Contact made. Welcome to Whacklow, Futtle, Crun and Bannister – Solicitors for Oaths, Thin Oil and Certain Thingsssssssssss.

MINNIE
Thingssssss!

Orchestra: All Join In 'Thingssssssssssss'.

CRUN
Thingssssssssss are catching onnnnnn, Min. Now Sir, what, apart from your plasticine nose, is the trouble?

NED
My wife left me.

CRUN
Where did she leave you?

NED
At home.

CRUN
What was her name?

NED
Mrs Seagoon.

CRUN
So, she's a married woman? There's a clue. Have you a description of her?

FX: Rustling of Plans

NED
Here's a complete set of plans of her.

CRUN
These are the plans of a house.

NED
She's inside.

FX: Door Opens

NED
Anybody in?

RAY (*off*)
Yes, there is.

CRUN
What is your name, Madam?

RAY
I can't see, the lights are fused.

FX: Door Closes

NED
You see? All we've got to do is find that house and there she'll be.

CRUN
Krermunck. Thingsssss . . . of Mongolia?

MINNIE (*off*)
I won't be a second.

CRUN
Good, there's no money in the boxing game. Min of Mongolia, this man in the mosquito net hat is a new client.

NED
How do you do.

MINNIE
I didn't catch the name.

NED (*dry*)
I haven't dropped it yet.

FX: Tubular Bell Dropped On Stage With A Telegraph Pole Clang

NED
That's it.

MINNIE
Mr. Steel, he's coming, he's coming neareer, he's almost here, he's arrived.

NED
Who?

MINNIE
Ha ha ha ha.

CRUN
Now, Ned, that will be a pound. Come and see us in ten guineas' time.

NED
Have you got change of a hern – no? Then to hell with you.

Grams: Wolf Howl

RAY
Man, that sounds like my cue and I don't like it, I don't like it at all.

The Ray Ellington Quartet: Music

WALLACE
That was Ray Ellington who is seven feet tall and covered in ginger hair, known in Woodside Park as – 'Gor, look at 'im!'. Part Three of 'Certain Thingssss'. Mr. Thynne – will you summarize?

THYNNE
The secret of Ned's missing home is simple. We have lifted it lock, stick and birrle on the back of a tank transporter. The dance inside continues. We intend to ransom the more important guests to Eastern Potentates, to be held as political hostages who will become the centre of international political tension at a reduced fee of ten guineas a day until World War Three, or the price of avocado pears is reduced to the ore fourteen minimum. Now for my next impression –

Grams: Tank Transporter Rumbling Along The Road

MORIARTY
Driving along the king's highwayyyyy.

THYNNE
Happy, Moriarty?

MORIARTY
Owwwwww.

THYNNE
Look, there's something in the road ahead.

MORIARTY
It *is* a head, with a body attached.

BLUEBOTTLE
It's mine, Bottle of Finchley. Can you give me a lift to London Town?

MORIARTY
Go on, hop it.

BLUEBOTTLE
It's too far to hop it.

ECCLES
Hullo, Bottle.

BLUEBOTTLE
Cor, look, look at him, in brown evening dress. Eccles of Lengths.

ECCLES
He's OK, Moriarty, he's a friend of mine. Come on.

BLUEBOTTLE
Ta, Eccles. Here's a cigarette card of Newt, and here's one of a King Edward potato at two months old.

ECCLES
Oh, just what I need for lunch (*Gulps*) Ohhhhh . . .

BLUEBOTTLE
I been doing life-guard duties on the Splon beach at Ratsgate.

ECCLES
I didn't know you could swim in water.

BLUEBOTTLE
I had to learn to swim at two weeks old.

ECCLES
Why?

BLUEBOTTLE
The vicar dropped me in the font.

Grams: Splash and Bubbles –

BLUEBOTTLE
– I went. My next impression will be of a goose.

Grams: Peter (Pre-Recorded): Screammmm

BLUEBOTTLE
Ohhhhh, hello everybody, I didn't see you there. One – two – three . . . oh, not such a big crowd tonight. (*Thinks, panic*) Is – is poor Bottle losing the public that has kept him in liquorice and long shorts for all these years? Am I a fallen idol? Another has-been? Noooooo! I shall go on from triumph to triumph.

FX: Swanee Whistle Down, and Thud Very Fast

BLUEBOTTLE
Oh, my trousers have come down! Never again will I trust knitted string from Freda Milge.

ECCLES
Never mind, have a brandy.

Grams: Long Pouring From A Three Gallon Tin Into A Glass. Then A Long Syphon of Soda

BLUEBOTTLE
No thank you. Ringgggg-ringgggg-ringgggg – the phoneeeeee. Hello?

NED
Hello, Bottle, help me, where is Robin's Post?

BLUEBOTTLE
It's on a lorry going down the Great North Road.

NED
You will be rewarded for this with a twill nightie and a spare sock. Gid up!

Grams: Dick Barton Theme – Then Paul Temple Theme – Then The Archer's Theme – Then Mrs. Dale's Harp

NED
It's pick of the flops! With that music behind me and my horse underneath –

Grams: Lone Ranger – William Tell Theme – Goes Under –

HERN
Yes, a fiery horse, a flash of light, two pounds of potatoes, a sack of knees and ho Silver and the Lone Ranger.

FX: Coconut Shells

NED
Gid up, proud beauty.

PETER (*old dear*)
All right, dear.

THYNNE
Ring ring ring in the direction of Ned.

NED
What's that? It sounds like a telephone. (*Tastes*) It tastes like a telephone. What number docs it taste like?

BLOODNOK
Hastings 1066.

NED
That's us. Hello?

MORIARTY (*distorted*)
Listen, Neddie, I'm warning you not to follow us. We've had beans for dinner.

NED
What what what? Arrest that phone, the man on the other end is a criminule.

FX: Handcuffs And Chains On Telephone

NED
There! Hello? Hello? Blast, he's escaped, this phone is empty. Tarara!

BLOODNOK
It's near enough for jazz.

NED
We'll never catch them on a horse. But, just as I said that, folks, an old Indian hooker drew up on a nearby canal.

LALKAKA
Hello hello hello hello, Mister Man.

BANAJEE
Yes, Hello. We are Hindu bargees, Lalkaka and Banajee Limited. Here is our card.

NED (*reading*)
Jim Jones and Tom Squat, Printers.

BANAJEE
Yes, they are the men we bought the cards from.

LALKAKA
We got them second hand.

NED
Right. Cast offfffff.

Orchestra: Open Sea Music: Shouts of 'Aye the Spon', etc.

NED
Now then, who's our navigator?

ECCLES
I am.

NED (*panic*)
Man the boatssssss! Neddie and children first.

ECCLES
Wait a minute . . . Major.

BLOODNOK
Let me explain. This man is brilliant at cartography and astral navigation – ask him any question. Eccles, did you know that the mouth of the Amazon is one hundred miles wide?

ECCLES
Oh, yer.

BLOODNOK
And the coast of Albania is ten thousand miles long?

ECCLES
Oh, yer.

BLOODNOK
You see? He knew the answer to both questions.

ECCLES
Yer, here's a map of the route.

NED
What's the scale.

ECCLES
Doh ray me far so la te doooooooooo.

NED
Perfect. (*Calls*) Set course for Ferpudden.

ECCLES
What's Ferpudden?

NED
Prunes and custard.

BLUEBOTTLE
Wind's coming up.

Orchestra: Ta Raaaaaa

BLOODNOK
Caught with their instruments down. Ohh, not long to the pay-off now, folks. Now, Neddie, pick a card – don't show it to me. What is it?

NED
Jim Jones and Tom Squat, Printers.

BLOODNOK
Correct.

JIM
Heloo, Jim, hello Jimmmmmm.

NED
Helooooo Jim.

JIM
Look what I found floating in the canal. – the pay-off.

NED
It's the front door of Robin's Post.

FX: Doop Opens

Grams: Old Fashioned Orchestra – As Beginning Of Story – Sound of Dancers

NED
Stop the music!

Grams: Slow Music Down To a Blur

NED
Where's my wife, Bulgarian Meg? Ahhh – Megggg – kis kis kis kisssss.

RAY
There *must* be some mistake.

PETER (*Meg the Bulgar*)
Neddie, Neddie darling, your back – your front – you brought them both with you.

NED
I carry them for sentimental reasons – I –

Grams: Great Avalanche Of Rocks

NED
She's fainted.

PETER (*doctor*)
Stand aside, I'm a doctor, I specialize in fainting. Groannnnnn.

FX: Body Falls To Ground

NED
So he does.

THYNNE
Neddie, you disrespectful swine – standing there with two fainted people – take your shoes off.

Grams: Two Small Explosions

THYNNE
Do you have to wear such loud socks?

NED
Yes, I've got deaf feet.

THYNNE
Yes, folks, exploding socks – it's the new noise clothes. Why not get your grannie a pair of red flannel drawers that go –

Grams: Great Cackling of Startled Hens

WALLACE
And with Lord Seagoon's wife safely fainted, and a good laugh on a pair of cackling drawers, we say farewell from page thirteen of another Goon Show.

BLOODNOK
Is there no end to it! Ohhhhh!

Orchestra: Old Comrades March